D0780318

3 Luchino Visconti

Geoffrey Nowell-Smith lectures in
Italian at Sussex University, and has
written widely on the Italian cinema
and on films in general, contributing to
Sight and Sound, *Afterimage*,
Twentieth Century Studies and other
periodicals. He is also co-editor and
translator of Gramsci's *Prison
Notebooks* and is currently working on a
history of Italian Marxism between
1890 and the present.

Luchino Visconti

Geoffrey Nowell-Smith

The Viking Press
New York

LIBRARY

FEB 1 2 1975

UNIVERSITY OF THE PACIFIC

291754

The Cinema One series is published by
The Viking Press in association with
the British Film Institute

Luchino Visconti by Geoffrey Nowell-Smith
first published by Secker & Warburg 1967
this edition, with additional material 1973
Copyright © Geoffrey Nowell-Smith 1967, 1973

All rights reserved

Published in 1973 in a hardbound and paperbound
edition by
The Viking Press, Inc.,
625 Madison Avenue, New York, N.Y. 10022

SBN 670-44426-X (hardbound)
SBN 670-01979-8 (paperbound)

Library of Congress catalog card number: 73-17729

Designed by Michael Farrell

Printed and bound in Great Britain

Contents

Introduction

Luchino Visconti belongs, with Welles and Resnais, to a select company of major directors whose international reputation was established early in their careers and has been maintained, on the basis of a relatively small output, ever since. Among his Italian contemporaries he is unique. Unlike Antonioni or Fellini he did not have to wait for recognition. Unlike Rossellini he has never been a prolific director, and has managed to concentrate his energies over quarter of a century on less than a dozen meticulously prepared productions. Unlike De Sica he has not degenerated as a director with the decline of the movement which first thrust him into prominence. His early films are now classics, and each new film he makes is an eagerly awaited cultural event. And yet he has remained obstinately impervious to changes in intellectual fashions. A lonely and unassailable giant, his work has a devious consistency paralleled, on the world scale, only by Fritz Lang and Orson Welles.

There are signs recently, however, that his hitherto impregnable reputation is now beginning to suffer a decline, and that he is paying the seemingly inevitable penalty for his refusal to go any way but his own. His career has always been bound up, in the public mind, with the Italian neo-realist movement. His position with regard to the movement was in fact equivocal. But so long as critical discussion was centred round the problems of a realist aesthetic, Visconti's films were always a key point of reference. He

7

has been seen, variously, as an embodiment of the committed and realist ideal, as its greatest betrayer, and as the man who most successfully transcended its limitations. Now that these problems no longer have the actuality they had ten, or even five years ago, Visconti's work has lost its particular exemplary role in the *Kulturkampf*. His latest films, though generally acknowledged, in a neutral fashion, as important and monumental works, have disappointed many people. They do not conform, somehow, to expectations built up on the basis of Visconti's past work. Nor do they break unexpectedly into the area where contemporary cultural battles are being fought.

What is happening to Visconti has happened before to other great directors. With Renoir in the 1940s it was a case of his films seeming to change and criticism being left behind. With John Ford, more recently, it could hardly be said that his films had changed, but the critical revolution brought about by the influence of *Cahiers du Cinéma* meant that he lost his place in the Pantheon in favour of different idols, from the same or from another generation. In both cases, however, a further turn of the wheel has restored them to their former position, though in a different guise. The liberal critique which put forward *La Grande Illusion* and *The Grapes of Wrath* as artistic and humanitarian ideals and neglected *French Can-Can* and *My Darling Clementine* has been superseded. The authors survive, but only on the basis of a thoroughgoing reappraisal of their work.

The principles which guided the revaluation of Ford and Renoir can now, I think, be legitimately and fruitfully applied to Visconti. It is not a question of reviving old polemics or laying down new dogmas, but of breaking down certain received ideas and establishing the basis of a more comprehensive interpretation. It is not possible to avoid polemic entirely, or even dogmatism. Misunderstandings still circulate, and demand to be contested. And, to a certain extent, the method of contesting them involves laying down, explicitly or implicitly, criteria of understanding which have to be taken as axiomatic.

The misunderstandings that require to be contested date back a

8

long way, to the problems raised by the neo-realist aesthetic in the 1940s. One way of getting round these problems would be to disregard them. At twenty years' distance the arguments are beginning to look a bit threadbare and out of date. Two things make this easy solution impossible. One is the persistence of part of the general aesthetic of neo-realism, its naturalism-with-a-social-conscience, in the minds of many people. The other is the undeniable fact of Visconti's connection with the movement and the need to produce a responsible redefinition of this connection. Visconti without neo-realism is like Lang without Expressionism and Eisenstein without Formalism—and without the Russian Revolution.

At the same time the most important job to be done remains that of liberating Visconti from the heritage of past polemics; to free his early work from the conventional and stultifying image of masterpieces of realism and his later work from the charge of being a degeneration from his former ideals. This does not mean exalting the later work at the expense of the earlier, but making it one's primary concern to consider the work as a whole, as the product of a single intelligence, and to seek out the connections between each film at whatever level they are to be found. In Visconti's case the connections are multifarious, and can be traced in his choice of actors, his use of décors, his concern with certain historical questions, and so on. The development of each film out of the problems posed by the last can also be easily demonstrated. But there are further links within his work which exist at a deeper level, less easily discernible, and which are perhaps even more important. It is these hidden structural connections which bind his work together and which combine to form a picture of the author and his work which is far more complex and interesting, as well as more coherent, than is generally imagined.

It is necessary, at this point, to make clear certain assumptions about the concepts of authorship and of structure which have guided me in this work. The so-called *auteur* theory can be understood in three ways: as a set of empirical assertions to the effect that every detail of a film is the direct and sole responsibility of its author, who is the director; as a standard of value, according to which every film that is a *film d'auteur* is good, and every film that is not is bad; and as a principle of method, which provides a basis for a more scientific form of criticism than has existed hitherto. The first interpretation is manifestly absurd. Any proponent of the theory who puts it forward uncompromisingly in that form both trivialises the theory and commits himself to a statement that is demonstrably untrue. The second is simply gratuitous and leads only to a purposeless and anti-critical aesthetic dogmatism. It is only in the third interpretation that the theory has any validity. As a principle of method the theory requires the critic to recognise one basic fact, which is that the author exists, and to organise his analysis of the work round that fact. Whether one is trying to get to grips with a particular film or to understand the cinema in general, let alone when one is studying the development of an individual director, the concept of authorship provides a necessary dimension without which the picture cannot be complete.

But the principle of authorship does not stop short here. If it were simply a recommendation to look at films in terms of their directors it would hardly be an advance on what we know already. However, one essential corollary of the theory as it has been developed is the discovery that the defining characteristics of an author's work are not always those that are most readily apparent. The purpose of criticism becomes therefore to uncover behind the superficial contrasts of subject and treatment a structural hard core of basic and often recondite motifs. The pattern formed by these motifs, which may be stylistic or thematic, is what gives an author's work its particular structure, both defining it internally and distinguishing one body of work from another.

The structural approach, which has evolved, by a kind of necessary accident, out of the applications of the *auteur* theory and resolves many of the difficulties of the theory as originally put forward, brings with it, however, problems of its own. It narrows down the field of inquiry almost too radically, making the internal (formal and thematic) analysis of the body of work as a whole the only valid object of criticism. In so doing it is in danger of neglecting

Visconti with Romy Schneider on the set of *Il Lavoro*

two other equally basic factors. One is the possibility of an author's work changing over time and of the structures being variable and not constant: the other is the importance of the non-thematic subject-matter and of sub-stylistic features of the visual treatment.

A completely structural approach to the work of a director seems to me at the present time unfeasible, except in very rare cases, of whom Visconti is not one. Despite the extreme formal and thematic consistency revealed in his films, the fact remains that he has changed and developed over the years. No single and comprehensive structure can be discerned, unchanging, underlying the whole of his work from *Ossessione* in 1942 to *Vaghe Stelle dell'Orsa* in 1965. Nor is he a director with whom the ostensible subject, in all its facticity, is a matter of no importance. He has carried over from *La Terra Trema* and the heritage of neo-realism, into his later films, a respect for the hard, intractable, documentary fact which cannot be assimilated into any simple analytic pattern. In most of his films the precise geographical and historical setting is as significant for our understanding of his work as the kind of themes that emerge from the story and the way it is told. Any analysis of his films, whatever its starting-point, is bound to take all these factors into account.

What I have preferred to do, therefore, rather than focus exclusively on elucidating the common underlying structures, is to consider the films singly, attempting in the analysis of each to bring out its relationship, hidden or overt, to the rest of Visconti's work. I have also dwelt at length, at the beginning of some chapters, on external factors: on the social and historical background in which the film is set; on the problems surrounding its production; and on the general "accidentalia" without which it would not have any substance. The arrangement of the book is dictated by these considerations. Basically it is chronological. But I have taken three films out of order so as to place them next to the work with which they most require to be compared—*Il Lavoro* with *Bellissima*, *The Leopard* with *Senso*, and *Vaghe Stelle dell'Orsa* with *White Nights*. The result of this shuffling exercise, as anyone who knows the order of Visconti's films will have realised, is to place at the end *Rocco and his Brothers*, Visconti's most ambitious and perhaps least satisfactory film. The reason for putting it last is partly negative: there didn't seem anywhere else to put it. But there is also another reason, which is that of all Visconti's films it is the one which most successfully defies analysis on purely internal criteria, and challenges the critic to look outside the narrow world of his private inquiry to problems which exist outside.

Postscript, 1972

Various changes have taken place since the above was written in 1967. In the first place, Visconti's reputation, so far from continuing to decline, is now once again, unaccountably, on the increase. In bringing the book up to date to include the three films—*Lo Straniero*, *The Damned*, and *Death in Venice*—completed by Visconti since 1966, I have decided to let the earlier part of the book stand exactly as it was originally written, despite the fact that the defence of Visconti's coherence as an *auteur*, which was part of the purpose of the original work, is no longer an urgent critical priority. It is also the case that his recent films have in a sense falsified part of my thesis on the relationship of realistic and melodramatic elements in his work. In these films certain features which had previously been kept in check emerge into the foreground, so that the overall trajectory of his career takes on a form different from the way I saw it five years ago. Meanwhile my own ideas have also changed. The new material included in this edition reflects both Visconti's change of direction and my change of vantage-point from which to view it. The revised judgement which I would now make of Visconti's work as a whole, together with the criticisms I have now of what I wrote in 1967, are implicit throughout the new section of the book and spelt out more explicitly at the end, on pp. 203–204.

1: Ossessione

Visconti's interest in the cinema developed late. At an age when Orson Welles was directing *Citizen Kane*, when Alexandre Astruc could complain that he was "already twenty-six and had not yet made *Citizen Kane*", and when most aspirant directors would be starting as documentarists or serving a long and laborious apprenticeship in the industry, Visconti was still living in seclusion and undecided about the future nature of his artistic interests. An accomplished musician, interested also in painting (interests which remain latent in his film work for a long time to emerge again more fully with *Senso* in 1954), his only foray into the world of spectacle was as set-designer for a play by G. A. Traversi in 1928. He was nearing thirty when in 1936 he left Italy with the intention of working in the cinema in England or France.

As luck would have it, and thanks to a chance meeting with Coco Chanel, he found himself, shortly after his arrival in France, attached to Jean Renoir's semi-permanent production team in charge of costumes and then as assistant director on *Une Partie de Campagne* and *Les Bas Fonds*.[1] In a recent interview on B.B.C. Television he has recalled this experience mainly in terms of what it meant to him politically, to escape from a Fascist country and to find himself working on equal terms with a group of left-wing enthusiasts, many of them Communists, in the heady atmosphere of the Popular Front. That this part of his experience had a lasting effect on him and helped to shape his future political commitment

14

there can be no doubt. What is harder to assess is Renoir's influence on him as an artist. There is an obvious, if superficial, analogy between aspects of Renoir's aesthetic in the 1930s and Italian neo-realism ten years later, just as there is between the French Popular Front and the post-war Italian left-wing bloc, to which Visconti belonged. Visconti's career seems therefore like a bridge between the two. But on a personal level the differences between the two artists are far more striking than the similarities. Visconti's debt to Renoir is mainly stylistic and is confined to one film, *Ossessione*, which he made during the war. After that, when Visconti begins to find his own feet and to establish an independent personality, all traces of Renoir's influence disappear. They are, however, present in *Ossessione*, in the method used to establish a character, in the relationship of character to landscape, in the use of a fluid and yet probing camera, and, on a more generic plane, in a shared debt to the naturalist tradition—in Renoir's case Maupassant and Zola, in Visconti's Giovanni Verga and Italian regional literature.

In 1940 it was Renoir's turn to come to Italy to make a film of *La Tosca* which was a cross between Sardou's original melodrama and Puccini's opera. For this film Visconti worked on the adaptation and then as assistant director. Renoir was not able to finish the film himself. He had just directed the opening sequences when Italy declared war on France, and Renoir left for the United States, leaving the film in the capable but uninspired hands of Charles Koch. Opinions differ on the subject of the finished film. In distant retrospect, Visconti regards it as mediocre and banal, falling far short of what he himself had envisaged and what Renoir might have made if he had stayed on. But something of *La Tosca*, whether echoes of the realisation or images of how he himself would have made the film, remained lodged in Visconti's imagination to appear in the making of *Senso*, the most "operatic" of Visconti's films, fourteen years later.

The problem which faced Visconti in 1954, with *Senso*, was that of going beyond the realist aesthetic. In the early 1940s, however, this was hardly yet an apposite question. What seemed necessary at the time was the opposite—to achieve some elementary form of realism in the context of a national cinema that was totally insipid and conformist. Visconti belonged, if only on the margins, to a kind of artistic resistance movement that was beginning to grow up round about 1940. The members of this movement, young critics and aspirant directors centred round the Cine-G.U.F. and the review *Cinema*, were all partisans, for political as well as aesthetic reasons, of a realistic cinema. Their literary idol was Verga, the great Sicilian late-nineteenth-century writer, and their ideal was a transcription into cinema terms of the naturalism, or more exactly *verismo*, of Verga's novels and stories. But behind all the references to tradition what most of them wanted, and some of them achieved, was something quite different. Not all of them (one thinks particularly of Michelangelo Antonioni) emerged as realists of any description, let alone *veristi* or *Vergani*. There was a certain confusion even in the literary references themselves. *Verismo* as a diffuse aesthetic fell as far short of realism as Verga, as an artist, rose above it. But intellectual confusion does not stop ideas from being influential, and one of the first people to undergo the influence of the prophets of neo-realism, and to translate their ideas into practice, was Visconti.

Ossessione, his first film, was produced in 1942, in an atmosphere of general disturbance. Italy was fighting, and beginning to lose, a war around the Mediterranean. Within months of the film being finished the Allied forces landed in Sicily and began working their way slowly through the Peninsula. The film did not emerge properly into the light of day until some years after the war, and then only in a severely mutilated and shortened version. As a result of these circumstances many legends have attached themselves to the story of the making of the film and an aura of mystification has come to surround its interpretation. The general purport of the legends is to bolster up the image of *Ossessione* as a precocious, maligned, and yet marvellous flower of the still inexistent neo-realist movement. Both in the legends and in the interpretation there is a nugget of truth. The film has origins in the cult of

Ossessione: Bragana and the priest

verismo and was to serve as an inspiration, of a kind, to later neo-realist production. But there is also a lot of legendary dross and more than a suspicion of critical alchemy in the proceedings. When the dross has been removed and the alchemy exposed *Ossessione* emerges as a very different, and furthermore a greater rather than a lesser film, than its first admirers would ever have claimed.

Given a chance to direct a film of his own, Visconti's first idea was a version of a short story by (significantly enough) Verga, *L'Amante di Gramigna*. When the project was refused by the censors he turned instead to a suggestion of Renoir's, an adaptation of an American thriller, James Cain's *The Postman Always Rings Twice*, which had already served as the basis for a French film in 1939 and was to be filmed again by Tay Garnett in Hollywood in 1946. The story, widespread but poorly documented, has it that the choice of Cain's novel as scenario was a subterfuge to deceive the Fascist censorship, which rubber-stamped the project as inoffensive on paper but was then horrified to see the most un-Fascist image of Italian life portrayed in the finished film, which transferred the action to an Italian setting. The censors then attempted to ban the film outright, but it was reprieved, so the story runs, only on personal instructions from the Duce himself.

This story, though somewhat inaccurate,[2] is quite significant. It manages at the same time to exalt Visconti as a crusader for the new realism and to denigrate him subtly by suggesting that this aristocratic dilettante had friends at court who gave him an influence and an escape route denied to lesser mortals. In fact Mussolini did not reprieve the film, and *Ossessione*'s troubles did not end with the end of Fascism. More important, just as the censorship difficulties which *Ossessione* encountered have been misrepresented as simply a question of Fascist politics (they involved the Church, *bien-pensant* opinion generally, commercial distributors, and even the American occupying forces), so Visconti's artistic intentions are simplified and belittled by the emphasis placed on the element of national realism in the adaptation.

Cinema criticism is often curiously nationalistic. While literary critics have acknowledged for a long time the profoundly renovating role played by American literature in the development of the Italian novel in the 1930s and 1940s, their cinema confrères have on the whole failed to recognise the debt of the Italian cinema to the same source—and to the American movies. It is partly the fact that in literature the connections are more obvious to the academic mind: Pavese wrote a thesis on Melville; Visconti did not write a thesis on Griffith. But there remains a strange reluctance to accept the obvious. The fiction persists that Visconti chose *The Postman Always Rings Twice* for no better reason than that it would not upset the censor and that the changes he made in his adaptation had no other purpose than to Italianise its indifferent theme. It never occurs to anyone to think that the story might have appealed to him precisely because it was American, and that he might have changed it not just to make it more Italian but to make it more Visconti. *Ossessione* certainly is very Italian, and it is also more realistic than Tay Garnett's film of the same novel. But there is a lot more to it than that.

Ossessione is a film about the destructive power of sexual passion. A man turns up by chance at a roadside country inn, stays on as a labourer and falls in love (or in desire) with the inn-keeper's wife and she with him. They decide to leave together, but after half an hour on the road she turns back and he goes away alone. A few weeks later the husband and wife encounter him again by chance in a near-by town and the husband, innocently, insists that he go back with them. On the journey the lovers, mainly at her instigation, murder the husband in a staged accident. They settle down uneasily to run the café. Unease and mutual mistrust grow when she collects on the old man's life insurance and he suspects her of having used him to wield the hatchet to serve her own financial purposes. In retaliation he spends an afternoon with another girl, but slips away when he realises that the police are closing in. The lovers are reconciled, but as they drive away to escape imminent arrest their car skids off the road and she is killed.

Melodramatic as this summary may sound, particularly the ending, it is not half so melodramatic as the novel or Tay Garnett's rather literal adaptation. Visconti has in fact purified the story line considerably, removing the elements of crude and even ridiculous poetic justice in which the novel abounded (such as having the man acquitted of the real murder but sentenced to death for the accident) and adding or expanding elements only in order to introduce an extra dimension of structural coherence behind the apparent arbitrariness of the plot. The arbitrary and accidental character of events and, even more, the arbitrariness of human (but not divine) justice is an important feature of the novel, and also appears, rationalised in a half-hearted and uncomprehending fashion, in the Garnett film. Visconti rejects it utterly. Tragedy in his films is never a trick of providence, and in *Ossessione*, as later in *Vaghe Stelle dell'Orsa*, the tragic outcome arises from the necessary logic of the situation into which the characters are thrown.

Turning Cain's parable of arbitrariness into a demonstration of necessity required, however, more than a simple alteration of plot mechanics. It meant creating a new structural framework in which to define the actions of the characters, and consequently making the characters themselves different. In the film the lovers, Gino and Giovanna, are both in different ways partial outcasts. They have an uneasy relationship with established society. They are neither totally integrated nor totally independent, and it is their inability either to be fitted in or to break loose that leads to their destruction.

Giovanna has had a tough time in the past. Her euphemistic phrase, "I used to get men to invite me to supper", contains an innuendo which is not difficult to grasp. Marriage, for her, to the superficially amiable but gross and uncomprehending Signor Bragana, was a last-ditch escape from a life of increasingly systematic prostitution; but it was an escape into slavery and mediocrity. Gino offers her passion and liberation, but on his terms, which to her are unacceptable. He proposes twice that they should leave together, and each time she hesitates. The first time, staggering ridiculously along the road in high heels, in the dust and heat, she is haunted by a fear of insecurity, and turns back. The second time, after the murder, it is not just a negative fear of insecurity that seizes hold of her, but positive ambition to enjoy, with Gino, a stability and comfort always denied to her. Despite Gino's pleas, she insists on staying on at the inn. She rejects the only life that Gino can offer her, and wants the one which society has always refused her and refuses her still. She even commits murder for the sake of it—a desperate and unproductive gesture, because from that moment she is a fugitive and an outcast. Only courage screwed to the sticking place, like that of Lady Macbeth, can keep her dreams alive.

Gino, for his part, has no such dreams of security and advancement. He is a wanderer, a passer-through, going from place to place and job to job as his fancy takes him. If he can have a woman with him on his travels, so much the better. He seduces the provocative Giovanna in total unawareness of the consequences to which her ambition will lead him. Although he loves her, he cannot change his way of life. When Giovanna goes back to her husband, he prefers to continue alone rather than return to a state of uneasy dependence at the inn. To be tied to a woman, and to a job, is bad enough. Under circumstances of permanent deceit, conducting a secret affair, it is intolerable.

After the murder, too, living openly with Giovanna in the gossipy village, he is afflicted with the desire to keep on the move, to escape from the inn, haunted to him by the memory of the dead husband, from people, particularly the priest, from the police, even (though it sounds a cliché) from himself. He comes to distrust even Giovanna, and is horrified by her delight when she learns about the insurance. He begins to be tormented by guilt and by a suspicion that he has been used for purposes alien to his own. The afternoon spent with the dancer, a relationship that is easy, human and, within self-imposed limits, satisfying and complete, is not only an act of spite against Giovanna (as such it would be rather futile), but a release from guilt, and almost, it seems, a return to nature and a cleansing purity.

The episodic figures, such as the dancer, are of key importance, both in themselves and the way they throw into relief the tormented character of Gino and Giovanna's liaison. The pattern of relationships is almost geometric, with Giovanna at a kind of epicentre, surrounded by but not connecting with the other characters. Psychologically, and as a person, she clearly *suffers* from this isolation, estranged from her husband and with Gino as her only life-line to the world outside. But it is doubtful if Visconti intended attention to be focused, in a psychological way, on her problems. In structural terms her isolation is to be seen rather as a *cordon sanitaire* which Visconti has drawn round her for his own purposes. Like Circe with the wanderer Ulysses, she entices Gino (significantly) by her singing:

> volsi Ulisse dal suo cammin vago
> al canto mio[3]

and having enticed him will not let him escape. Unlike Circe, she succeeds in destroying him, even though at the very end, in a literal sense, he destroys her.

Giovanna, then, is isolated. Gino, however, is not, and in his relations with the other, episodic characters one finds portrayed the counter-image which Visconti puts forward to the guilty and destructive passion in which the lovers are consumed. Apart from the dancer, whose role has been discussed above, by far the most important of these is the strange figure of Lo Spagnuolo—"The Spaniard", the solitary travelling showman whom Gino meets on the train after leaving Giovanna, and who more or less picks him up by an offer to pay the penniless Gino his fare. It is a gesture of implicit and intuitively recognised solidarity between men and between wanderers, and contrasts sharply with Giovanna's trick to hold Gino back at the beginning of the film, when she sends her husband after him on the false pretext that he has not paid for his meal. Between Gino and the Spagnuolo, on the other hand, there is a mysterious and spontaneous *accord*, and the scenes between them receive a lyrical expansion which the scenes between Gino and Giovanna, with the possible exception of the scene at the end when he learns that she is pregnant, do not have. The only point of tension between the two men comes when the Spagnuolo discovers that Gino's suitcase is full of women's clothes, evidence of Gino's betrayal both of true male comradeship (the Spagnuolo is

Ossessione: Gino and the Spagnuolo

a homosexual) and of the wanderer's basic rule to form no attachments. But this is not enough to destroy their friendship. That happens only towards the end, when the Spagnuolo traces Gino back to the inn, after the murder, and tries to get him back. Gino is obdurate. In a fit of anger he knocks the other man down. When a detective who is shadowing the lovers latches on to the Spagnuolo, the latter shrugs him off and goes his own way.

The Spagnuolo has so often been interpreted as a "positive hero" that it is worth making one or two points against this simplified interpretation. The first is that in the full version of the film there is an enigmatic scene at the end when the Spagnuolo calls on the police and apparently completes the cycle of betrayals by tipping them off against Gino. The second is that one should not confuse a character with the role he is called on to play in the structure of the work. In the nineteenth-century novel, where the two are synonymous, or in the theatre of Brecht, where the distinction is explicit and essential, this confusion would not arise. But with Visconti it can and does, and should be clarified. As a character the Spagnuolo is ambiguous and not altogether agreeable, and he is a law unto himself and consistent with himself. Structurally he has two distinct and conflicting roles, independent of his personality: to point to the existence of what, in Visconti's eyes, is a positive alternative to the destructive passion of Gino and Giovanna, and to round off the cycle of betrayal. Neither action invalidates the significance of the other.

The theme of betrayal is important. It recurs in various forms in many of Visconti's films, notably in *Senso*, which *Ossessione* most clearly foreshadows. Like that of the roles performed by the characters, this theme has a double significance. On the one hand, taken in isolation, it emerges as a permanent item of Visconti's thematic concerns, a part of his universe. But it also has a more specific function in the dynamics of the plot. In *Ossessione* each relationship is seen, at least by one of the parties, as an exclusive commitment and as conferring obligations. This is true not only of Bragana's assumptions about marriage, but of Giovanna's feelings about her *grand amour* and the Spagnuolo's attitudes to

Ossessione: Gino with Anita and Giovanna

comradeship and the life on the road. By this token Gino brings about his own ruin. He ignores or despises the claims made on him by Giovanna and the Spagnuolo and is fully himself only in the undemanding relationship with Anita. In other words, he is incapable of making a full commitment to a person or a way of life—a fact which explains, though it does not cause, his inadaptation to society. But the role of betrayals does not stop here, nor is it all the result of Gino's indifference. Apart from the Spagnuolo's *coup de grâce* there are also the adultery and the murder, both of which are, in a wide sense, acts of betrayal, and both of which Gino feels guilty about, not only because murder is murder but because Bragana is, after all, a friend, even if the friendship was mainly on the older man's side.

The static pattern of *Ossessione*, then, is one in which easy love is shown as preferable to guilty passion and male comradeship as an alternative to either. Passion, particularly sexual, is a disorder which draws the victim out of relation with a society which cannot accommodate him, and then destroys him. Betrayal is a permanent threat, part of the general instability of human relations. This is a pattern which will recur again later and is here clearly announced for the first time. But every bit as interesting as the static pattern is the way things are actually worked out in context, the way for instance that each relationship is formed by impulse or accident and then terminated by an act of betrayal, or the way the narrative receives its formal articulation.

The first striking thing about this formal articulation is how simple it is, and how conventional. The form is that traditional to classical theatre and opera, a series of scenes involving two or at most three people at a time. This formal articulation reflects (or determines; the two are inseparable) the structure and development of the relations between characters, who form a series of couples. Leaving aside the marginal couples—priest/husband, husband/Gino—the main development is expressed in the progression Bragana/Giovanna, Giovanna/Gino, Spagnuolo/Gino, and Gino/Anita, or (more simply still) Bragana—Giovanna—Gino-Anita. The movement is linear and progressive, away from the stable world of marriage and village life towards a more fluid existence. But it cannot be consummated. The forces of the past and of society are too strong. Gino is drawn back to Giovanna, and, sweeping round in a wider circle to block all escape routes, the police close in.

This linear pattern closed off with a couple of loops at the end is much tidier than the rambling original. But it represents a very tentative stage in Visconti's development. His later films have a much tighter construction which respects much more the complexity of social bonds, and where the pattern remains linear, as in *Rocco and his Brothers*, it has a much more positive trajectory. Part of the explanation for this lies in the adaptation from a genre, the thriller, whose postulates Visconti does not share, and part in the form of social life described. The significance of this can best be brought out by looking at the role played by the police in *Ossessione*.

The police in *Ossessione* are an extrinsic force whose only role is to give a conventional ending to the story. They represent an abstract justice which has no reality within the concrete world of the film until it suddenly imposes itself at the end. In Visconti's later films where the police and "justice" have a role to play, this role is always more closely integrated. In *La Terra Trema* the police is an oppressive presence right from the start. In *Senso* the Austrian military justice into whose hands Franz is betrayed by Livia is part of the political structure made explicit throughout the film and an aspect of the code which Franz evades and rebels against in his love for Livia. In *Rocco and his Brothers*, finally, the handing over of Simone to the police by Ciro consummates a movement away from the close self-contained world of the primitive family to the world of bourgeois society and the State, and as such has a relatively progressive function. In a film deliberately as loosely structured as *Ossessione* these considerations cannot apply, while at the same time the cops are not what they usually are in thrillers. As a result they remain detached.

The detached role of the police is an element of a general cultural dissociation in the world of *Ossessione* and the way it is described. Gino passes through this world without settling and there is in any case not much of a world to belong to. Bragana's sentimental attachment to army life and the images of the priest strapping shotgun and cartridges round the *soutane* are added touches which help to establish the sense of cultural dissociation. This again contrasts with Visconti's later preference for self-contained cultural environments such as families. It is also crucial to an understanding of his attitude to realism and to the neo-realist movement.

Stylistically, *Ossessione* is the most realistic of Visconti's films. At the same time it cannot be called, without qualification, a work of neo-realism. It is visually naturalistic in its use of natural locations, presented with a minimum of expressive distortion. It is also rooted in a naturalistic conception of character, and places character in landscape in a way which is generally unaffected but does not exclude certain sophisticated expressive effects. One thinks notably of the scene of Bragana and the lovers at the singing contest, which has a quite extraordinary similarity to Flaubert's description of the *comices agricoles* in *Madame Bovary*. Most importantly it excludes explicit moral and political judgments but approaches its subject from the point of view of the participants in the action. Like the other feature observed, the general cultural dissociation is just a fact about the setting: it is not explicitly significant.

These realistic features were what most caught the attention of critics when the film first appeared—fairly enough, since the version most people saw had been shorn of those scenes, particularly the episodes with the Spagnuolo, which were most likely to contradict this impression. The fact that, as we have seen, the interest of *Ossessione* is by no means exhausted by the realism of its approach, does not mean that its stylistic realism is not significant—particularly in view of the time it was made. But this is not enough to justify the enthusiastic paean of Antonio Pietrangeli (who had, incidentally, worked on the film and ought to have seen a bit deeper) to the effect that with the first shot of Gino asleep on a lorry neo-realism was born.

Ossessione: Gino, arriving and departing

"Allons-nous baptiser nous-même le Gino d'*Ossessione*?
Nous pouvons l'appeler, voulez-vous, le néo-réalisme italien."[4]

This is just sheer, indiscriminate mystification.

One of the most interesting features of *Ossessione* is its lack of political and historical perspectives. This in itself is sufficient to mark it off from almost all Visconti's later films on the one hand and the bulk of neo-realist production on the other. Historical judgment is an integral part of *Senso*, *Rocco and his Brothers*, *The Leopard*, and *Vaghe Stelle dell'Orsa*, and the inclination to take up a political stance is obvious enough in De Sica and early Rossellini, not to mention out and out political directors like De Santis. What one must bear in mind here are the circumstances in which the various directors worked and their films were made. The political circumstances of the years 1943–50 allowed and indeed called out for direct artistic treatment. Political content and unequivocal commitment imposed themselves naturally, in the post-war situation, even on Rossellini, and without this impetus neo-realism would not have acquired its specific character. In Rossellini's case his interest in the immediate realistic representation of actions and events attached itself to a situation that was one hundred per cent political, in which political action was immediate to an exceptional degree. But this connection between realism and political commitment was contingent on certain particular unrepeatable events. Rossellini has remained a realist, but the focus of interest has changed with the movement of time.

Visconti too has changed, though in a different direction. Whereas with Rossellini a realistic and immediate treatment of something for which he feels a direct interest uneasily masks a set of fairly constant moral imperatives, with Visconti there are no imperatives, realism appears as incidental and direct interest expresses itself only in the form of certain recurring themes and motifs. Their paths coincided very little: first in the general concern of any artist for the truth of a situation, real or imagined; and secondly in their brief association with a moment of social realism in the Italian cinema. Even in this association the tangents never

30

Ossessione: the death of Giovanna

quite touched, and their paths have since diverged a lot further—Visconti to become more profoundly political but stylistically less of a realist, and Rossellini to become an apparent political opportunist but morally and aesthetically consistent with what he has always been.

There is no need to complicate the picture further by referring to the careers of other directors who passed through the neo-realist experience, but if one were to do so one would find a similar pattern of brief convergence round a diffuse blob on the film-historical map. To characterise neo-realism is in fact extremely difficult, except as regards when it happened. If a social and aesthetic definition were to be attempted, in terms say of five qualities fairly generally accepted as characteristic—realistic treatment, popular setting, social content, historical actuality, and political commitment—one would not find many films which satisfy all these conditions together. What one can point to, however, and for our purposes it is sufficient, is the general convergence of a number of Italian directors at a particular time round some at least of the qualities proposed as the norm. Once the general area has been delimited the trajectory of each director becomes easier to plot.

The trajectory of Visconti's career sweeps in a wide arc round the area generally known as neo-realism. *Ossessione* is pre-neo-realist; it anticipates certain of the themes and styles that were to become the stock-in-trade of the movement, but, for good historical reasons, necessarily misses out on others. It is, one might say, realism without the neo-. Then, for six years, he does not make another film, and when he does, with *La Terra Trema*, it sets him moving on a new path, away from neo-realism altogether.

NOTES

1. See Gaston Bounoure in *Premier Plan*, numéro spécial 22-23-24; *Jean Renoir*, ed. Bernard Chardère, pp. 293–4.
2. For a more accurate version, see Marcel Martin, fiche on *Ossessione*, in *Image et Son*, no. 120, March 1959.
3. Dante, *Purgatorio*. xix, 22.
4. Antonio Pietrangeli, *La Revue du Cinéma*, 13 May 1948.

2: La Terra Trema

One of the most remarkable features of Visconti's career, which marks him off quite clearly from most of his neo-realist contemporaries and which has not on the whole been fully appreciated by the critics, is his apparent indifference to burning issues of actuality. The real heart of the neo-realist movement was the Resistance film and the often agonisingly direct contact it re-established between the spectator and recent events, and the decline of the movement can be traced to the moment when this genre lost its immediacy and became at best reflective, at worst sentimental. Visconti's only contribution to the vital heart of the movement was the short episode he directed for the compilation film, *Giorni di Gloria*, under the general direction of Mario Serandrei, in 1945 (see Filmography). After that he does not mention the Resistance, the war, or its aftermath directly for another twenty years, when he returns to the subject in a distant and devious manner in *Vaghe Stelle dell'Orsa*.[1] This remoteness is characteristic. Visconti's career has many paradoxes, but it has a consistent base, a constant reflective concern with certain fundamental problems related both to his own personal situation and to the historical development of Italian society as a whole. Not all the aspects of this concern emerged at once. Some, such as his historical interests, developed later. Others, particularly the more intimate, were stifled at a time when the prevailing current in the Italian cinema was towards an almost documentary conception of cinematic realism. In this period the

most striking influence of Visconti's personal situation on his work was the protection it afforded him. Aristocratic, temperamentally aloof, conscious of the advantages and anomalies of his privileged position, he remained unaffected by the general atmosphere of passionate out-going concern for immediate questions in which so many of his contemporaries were caught up. His detachment from immediate concerns did not prevent him from absorbing the serious content of the aesthetic-political agitation that was going on around him, but he drew his own lessons from it and his Marxist commitment was different in kind from the diffuse leftism of many of his colleagues. It had its source in a sense of history, and of his personal situation in the historical process, rather than in sentiment, and it expressed itself in historical reflection mediated by a sense of artistic form, rather than in the more obvious forms of propaganda which provide the surface gloss of the neo-realist movement.

The chiselled beauty of its images, the simplicity and rigour of its narrative, and its unbending concern with social realities have all caused *La Terra Trema* to be hailed as a masterpiece of the propaganda film. But this simplistic appreciation is belied both by the story of how Visconti came to make it and by its lack of impact on an ill-prepared public. *La Terra Trema* is not, either in intention or in effect, a work of propaganda. It is a great film, but not a flawless masterpiece, and the reasons for both its greatness and its limitations are far more complex than is usually made out. From the choice of subject-matter to the final presentation of the finished film, *La Terra Trema* is riddled with complexities and difficulties. To endorse it or to reject it for its propagandist aspect alone is an evasion of almost the issues raised by the film.

The first difficulty lies in the choice of subject-matter—the Southern question—and in Visconti's approach to it. The Southern question is a permanent running sore in the body politic of Italy. All the great social and political changes which have taken place in Italy since unification have been generated and have had their effect largely in the North. To these changes the South contributed very little, and gained from them even less. No better served by Fascism

La Terra Trema: 'Ntoni
La Terra Trema: Aci-Trezza →

than it had been by any previous régime, the South did not even enjoy the benefits of the Resistance in 1943–5. In the place of a spontaneous political upsurge, the South experienced only invasion and the return of banditry and the Mafia. The year 1945 found the South, and Sicily in particular, in the same state of poverty, apathy, primitivism, and corruption, which had struck and horrified observers of the Southern question at the time of unification eighty years before.

Apart from simple indifference and *laissez-faire*, two forms of possible solution have been put forward to the problems of the South. One is based on the idea of massive intervention by the central government to stamp out banditry and corruption, to reform the system of land tenure and to introduce industry. The second, deriving from Gramsci, envisages a radical transformation of Southern society from within, connected with a mass political movement allying the Southern peasants with the industrial workers from the North. The highly political atmosphere of Italy in the 1940s made it impossible for a film-maker to approach the Southern question without some bias towards one or other of these political solutions to the problem.

On the other hand, the concentration of political and cultural activity in the North, which in 1947 was still the scene of reprisals and *règlements de comptes* between ex-Fascists, Communists, and the rest, meant that it was exceptional for the South to receive any attention at all. Visconti was one of the first neo-realist directors to turn his attention towards the South and to Sicily, the most Southern (or the most un-Northern) region of all. Another was Pietro Germi (*In Nome della Legge*, 1948). But whereas Germi started from a reformist standpoint and further compromised his intentions by coming (albeit under pressure) to an arrangement with the Mafia,[2] Visconti adopts from the outset a position of total revolutionary intransigence, and though forced to abandon one of the political premisses on which his original project was based, remains intransigent to the end. This intransigence, aesthetic even more than political, is what gives the film the elemental quality that has always struck and sometimes dumbfounded critics. But it also serves as a mask behind which the subtleties, complexities, and occasional inconsistencies of the film remain tucked away and hidden from view.

In 1947, Visconti went to Sicily, with a small amount of capital advanced by the Communist Party, to make what was initially to have been a short documentary. He stayed there for six months, and the project gradually expanded in scale until what was proposed became a mammoth epic on the conditions of the poor workers and peasants and their struggle to liberate themselves from oppression. The film was to consist of three interlinked episodes, dealing with the fishermen, the peasants, and the workers in the sulphur-mines. As things turned out only one episode, that on the fishermen, was ever finished, and that in a form radically different from originally envisaged. It is this episode, which still bears the sub-title "Episodio del Mare", that is known in Italy and abroad under the general title of *La Terra Trema*.

Visconti brought to the project a great amount of revolutionary fervour, and an even greater ignorance of actual conditions. The whole project can be fruitfully compared to Eisenstein's equally grandiose and even less successful *Que viva Mexico!* Like *Que viva Mexico!*, *La Terra Trema* suffered from being abstractly conceived and unrealisable from the outset. Even (which was unlikely) if Visconti had received full co-operation from his producers and financiers, he could never have made the film as originally conceived. The contradiction was too great between what he wanted and what was there for him to see. Like Eisenstein, Visconti arrived on the scene as an outsider with the idea of making a film that would be at the same time a document and a call to arms. Convinced (apparently) that the hour of revolution had come, he envisaged a dramatic exposé of the conditions of perpetual humiliation suffered by the exploited Sicilian masses, which would resolve itself in a grand finale in which the solidarity of all the oppressed would bring at least partial victory.

It is easy to be sarcastic at the expense of Visconti's political *naïveté*, but it is beside the point. The scenario for the first version, which was published in *Bianco e Nero* some years later,[3] represents only a very early draft, which would in any case have been modified later as scenarios always are. What is interesting here is not so much the political as the aesthetic premisses from which Visconti started out. If the function of art is revolutionary (which, in a revolutionary period, is not an absurd premiss), and revolution was on the cards at any moment (which, from a Northern point of view, it certainly seemed to be), then a film on this pattern could fulfil its function by anticipating the cause it set out to further. Unfortunately, even in the balmy perspectives of 1947, the project was beset by contradictions. In the first place, the Sicilian proletariat was not going to rise, *en bloc*, against its oppressors, and if it did it was going to fail. The forces of reaction were too entrenched. An uprising would not develop into a revolution. The political premiss was therefore false.

Given even that the political premiss might have been true, there would still be something odd about a man of Visconti's temperament indulging in this sort of political wish-fulfilment, were it not clear from his later films that the initial formation of an abstract and often highly politicised schema is an integral part of his method of work. His initial scenarios have an ideological clarity and purity about them which is then systematically betrayed in the final elaboration. This betrayal can take various forms, some fruitful, some not. Here in *La Terra Trema* it takes the form of abandoning a totally unworkable discipline and reshaping the film in accordance with objective demands. The documentary moment prevails over the ideological. Resisting the temptation to turn the village of Aci-Trezza into the location for an imaginary revolution, which would have been a total violation of the reality of a film conceived first and foremost as a document, Visconti recast his story in a more pessimistic and "realistic" form.

In the final version of *La Terra Trema* as realised and distributed abroad the story is made to follow the basic outlines of the plot of Verga's *I Malavoglia*, the classic novel of Sicilian life and conditions which provided part of the original inspiration for Visconti's shift of interest towards the South. This derivation is important. Even in their periods of greatest originality Italian cultural forms have always been consciously derivative, drawing alternately on models provided by the native tradition and on the fruits of innovation elsewhere. Italian literature in particular has also been characterised by a constant tension between more classicising and rhetorical modes of expression and a more realistic vein of inspiration. In so far as neo-realism, both in literature and in the cinema, represented a reaction against the classicistic and rhetorical stance adopted by artists in the Fascist period, its models tended to be those of American realism of the 1930s and, of course, Verga. It was the interaction of these models which, in the early 1940s, helped to produce *Conversazioni in Sicilia* and *Ossessione*, as well as a whole host of lesser books and films. But the forms of naturalism and *verismo*, derived from Verga and Renoir, which were fundamental to *Ossessione*, are absent from *La Terra Trema*. Verga's influence stops short at the level of an initial inspiration and a convenient story, while Renoir seems to be forgotten entirely. The cinematic models for *La Terra Trema* are Flaherty and Eisenstein.

The influence of the incongruous tandem of Flaherty and Eisenstein is mainly stylistic and will be referred to later. The question of Visconti's debt to Verga is of more immediate relevance, because it shows the same tensions at work as does the difference between scenario and realisation.

Verga's story concerns the struggle of a fishing family, led by its aged and conservative grandfather, to eke a sufficient living out of a hostile sea to enable them to keep their roots on land, symbolised by the old family home. The world of the novel is one completely dominated by necessity, in which society and social laws are a superstructure in a hierarchy of oppression, underlain by the direr laws of inanimate nature. The Malavoglia do not in any real sense revolt against this oppression. Such *hubris* is hardly admitted even as a logical possibility, let alone a reality. They suffer, and they survive. The unchanging laws which govern their existence continue unchanged.

Needless to say, this pessimistic and fatalistic vision of things could have no place in Visconti's original schema for the film. Even in the finished version, where Visconti reverts to Verga's story, the underlying vision is very different. *La Terra Trema* in its finished form offers the first evidence of a creative and dialectical tension that is characteristic of much of Visconti's work, between a deeply rooted pessimistic fatalism and a more optimistic intellectual conception of the possibilities of human action. In *La Terra Trema* it is the voluntaristic optimism that dominates. But the other pole continues to exert an attraction, emphasised by the reversion to the plot of *I Malavoglia*. If it was largely the experience of objective conditions which forced Visconti to modify his original plan, there was also a strong emotional undertow at work, determining the direction in which the modifications were made.

In the film, as in the book, the fishermen are defeated. But the circumstances and above all the consequences of their defeat are no longer the same. Their enemy is not the sea, against which they pit themselves in the miserable struggle for survival, but the exploitation by other men which forces them to undertake the struggle in the first place. Without the capital to own or equip the boats they go out in or the organisation to market the meagre haul of fish they bring in each morning, they are utterly dependent on the wholesalers who own the boats and pay the fishermen a derisory price for their catch. The Valastro, who are incidentally not one of the poorest families, for they own their own house and can afford to take on day-labourers to help work the boat they hire, attempt to escape from this oppression. They mortgage their house and attempt to set up an independent business with the proceeds. But the need to recoup their initial financial outlay forces them to go out to sea at all times and in all weathers, and one night they are caught in a storm and the boat is destroyed and with it their entire livelihood. The mortgage is foreclosed and the Valastro are left with nothing, except the possibility of working as *braccianti* on other families' boats.

For the Valastro defeat is total and irremediable. But the future of the fishermen is not eternally fixed and crystallised in the failure of a single family to overcome oppression alone. The film is centred round two key episodes, each of which represents a stage in the development of the consciousness of the young 'Ntoni Valastro. In

La Terra Trema: 'Ntoni throwing the scales into the sea

the first, disgusted at the miserable prices being offered for the night's catch, 'Ntoni leads a spontaneous revolt of the fishermen against their oppressors. The wholesalers' scales, symbol of exploitation, are thrown into the sea and their owners after them. The police are called in and "order" is restored. 'Ntoni is carted off to prison, but released amid general jubilation a few days later. It is at this point that 'Ntoni realises that the source of their oppression lies, not in the necessary world of nature, but in the arbitrary world of social exploitation, and that he takes the decision that, if nobody else will follow them, he and his family will go it alone. The second comes after the defeat and immiseration of the Valastro, when 'Ntoni is walking along the shore and comes across the wreckage of his old boat being put together and recaulked for another family to use. There is a small girl sitting by the boat and 'Ntoni talks to her. Here, next to a relic of past disaster and talking to someone whose life lies in the future, 'Ntoni articulates for the first time the lesson of his defeat: the failure of any individual attempt to go it alone, and the need for collective and concerted action if exploitation is to be brought to an end and the future secured.

Basically what Visconti has done is to rewrite Verga in the light of Marx. He has shifted the focus of interest from the old grandfather to the young and active 'Ntoni, and from the house, to which, in the novel, the family were sentimentally and conservatively attached, on to the boat, on which the Valastro pin their hopes for the future, and he has placed the emphasis on the family's active attempts to throw off social exploitation. This procedure was not without its dangers. It could easily have meant, for example, the replacement of one abstract schema (Verga's quasi-scientific naturalism) with another more abstract still—a patina of vulgar-Marxist clichés and half-truths. There were dangers also of slipping into miserabilism on the one hand and vague affirmations of abstract humanism on the other. What saved him from these dangers (but led him into others, as we shall see) was the way in which his preconceived interpretative model fused and interpenetrated with actual Sicilian experience during the making of the film. It is not imposed on a recalcitrant reality but emerges from that reality in the form of the consciousness that the fishermen acquire of their situation through their own actions, while an idea of the sort of actions the fishermen would be likely to undertake was provided to Visconti by the fishermen themselves. The essential mediation is to be found in the character of 'Ntoni, who embodies the new consciousness and in whom this consciousness grows as a result of a series of extremely concrete determinations which are worth examining in some detail.

At the beginning of the film 'Ntoni is courting Nedda, the daughter of a relatively well-to-do family in the village. But Nedda's family will not give her (and her dowry) away to a poor family like the Valastro. At the same time 'Ntoni is faced with heavy responsibilities at home. His father is dead, a victim of the sea, and the grandfather is too old to work and too worn down by years of oppression to do anything but shake his head at the thought of innovation and initiative. 'Ntoni is therefore precociously in the position of head of the family, young, impetuous, and lacking guidance. Possibilities for advancement spiral above his head. If he is to marry Nedda, his family must first improve their economic and social position. But once he marries her that new position will be secured. His marriage to Nedda becomes a matter of his responsibility to his family, and buying the boat a response not simply to a generalised awareness of exploitation but to the particular claims of his own sexuality and his family's needs.

Similar factors affect the family's rise and slide into ruin. One of 'Ntoni's sisters is being eyed by a young labourer. When the Valastro become independent, he turns away from her, despite her protestations, because he knows better than she that she is now unattainable to him. When the family falls it is too late and he does not come back. The other sister has flirted (innocently enough, by Northern standards) with a stranger, a would-be Don Juan from the police station. So long as the family are independent this is supportable, but after the disaster traditional values reassert themselves. The family cannot stand the humiliation implied by what she has done or allowed to happen, and she is driven out.

45

Meanwhile Grandfather is dead, and 'Ntoni's brother Cola, despairing of the future at home, has yielded to the blandishments of a mysterious stranger and has emigrated to the North. This means that by the time that 'Ntoni reaches his second *prise de conscience* the family has disintegrated. Liberated from the responsibilities that led him to take his first disastrous decision he is able to see beyond them and to project himself into a world unfettered by traditional concerns.

It is in the choice of concrete and immediate determinations that Visconti reveals most clearly his own artistic personality. No motives in Visconti's films are ever shown as unmixed, abstract, or "pure"; all are mixed and many are confused. In the later films, as we shall see, this takes the form of a constant association of sex with violence, of violence with sadism, of love with possession, and marriage with economics. Lucidity consists in unravelling the strands, and acting consciously in the light of what you expect to be the consequences, rather than blindly in response to a confused pressure. Very few of Visconti's characters attain this ideal. In *La Terra Trema*, where the area of confusion is more restricted (the element of sexual violence for example is entirely absent), 'Ntoni wins through to understanding. He and Don Fabrizio in *The Leopard* are in fact the only Visconti characters to do so without losing their humanity. But in order for 'Ntoni to reach this stage he must first lose everything, including the power to act. Pessimism reasserts itself. The owl of Minerva, in Hegel's words, begins its flight when the dusk is falling.

Visconti's approach remains, therefore, ultimately reflective, and inward rather than outward looking. At a certain point, which is when 'Ntoni becomes conscious but is impotent to act, the dialectic runs out. No further advance is possible. 'Ntoni has gone as far as he can go within the confines of the village. The way forward is not stated, but it is for 'Ntoni to follow his brother Cola and get out. This is to become the starting-point for *Rocco and his Brothers*. But within the context established by the film it is hardly an immediate possibility. What is immediate and real is the world of the village of Aci-Trezza, a world isolated and caught up in itself, which holds

Visconti's imagination and confines it as surely as it limits and confines 'Ntoni.

The isolation of the village is underlined by the fact that, for the whole two and three-quarter hours that the film lasts, the camera never leaves it for a moment. It never strays beyond the line of the hills and the offshore rocks which mark the confines of the fishermen's world. When 'Ntoni is taken to prison, the camera records his arrest and his arrival back in the village, but not the journey, the prison, or the trial. It records the presence of strangers, like the mysterious character in knee-breeches who comes to persuade some of the young men to emigrate, or the grand lady who arrives to take part in a ceremony of dedication for a new boat: but it does not say where they come from or who they are. It shares the viewpoint of the fishermen, for whom all visitors are strangers and, by implication, not merely strangers but strange. The major institutions of society are also seen as alien—or else are absent entirely. There are no political parties, no trade unions. The police are marked off from the rest of the community by their uniforms, their voices, their large size, and the imposing appearance of the building from which they operate. There are churches and church bells and priests, but they are a physical rather than a social presence. Only when a storm whips up and the storm bell is rung and the women huddle on the steps does the church become real. But its reality is like that of the rocks that guard the entrance to the harbour, a symbol of permanence, but suggesting, unlike the rocks, permanent security as well as permanent fear.

In some of the more purely pictorial images—the storm, the overcast and sultry sky, the black-shawled women scurrying to and fro—and in the shots of impassive weather-beaten faces, there is a straight emotional charge that is reminiscent of Eisenstein. The cutting too is crisp and rhythmic, though there is no systematic use of the associative montage characteristic of Eisenstein's early films. The use of images and of the cutting between them is in fact pictorial rather than narrative or conceptual. The effect aimed at, and achieved, is a form of pictorial realism which is occasionally at odds with the analytical tone of the exposition.

The source of the conflict lies in the problem of language. The natural speech of the inhabitants of Aci-Trezza is not Italian but a dialect, and moreover a dialect which, because of the isolated position of the village, is well-nigh incomprehensible not only to continental Italians but to most other Sicilians as well. Partly through practical necessity (the villagers could not be taught to speak their dialogues in standard Italian) and partly for the sake of realism, the entire soundtrack of the film was shot in dialect and then overlaid with an Italian commentary explaining the events and what was being said. The pictorial style of the film was matched to the dialogue to form an audio-visual whole, while the more analytical content of the film was supplied by the commentary. This division of the film into a conceptual element and an element of "pure" (i.e. pictorio-musical) cinema was a necessary conclusion of Visconti's search for complete realism. But it was a conclusion that brought him straight up against an impasse.

Considered simply as a technique the juxtaposition of the two levels is not necessarily an aid to realism at all. It does nothing to solve the problem of content, whether of the images or of the text, nor does it prescribe any necessary relation between the two. In the only case I know of where exactly the same technique was used—Josef von Sternberg's *The Saga of Anatahan*—the effect is one of total and intentional irrealism. The problem is of course most obvious in documentary, but it affects fiction films as well. It is posed most acutely in Marker's *Lettre de Sibérie*, where the same images are made to bear three different, and conflicting, commentaries. But it has also been faced by Jean Rouch, in his attempts to integrate the anthropological observer into the fabric of his accounts, and by Godard in *Une Femme Mariée*. Each of these directors has found a different solution, but each has been forced, in one way or another, to admit the impossibility of a strictly objective form of realism unmediated by the intrusion of any form of subjectivity. Visconti's solution (or non-solution) is similar to that of Flaherty. It is an anthropological cinema in which the anthropologist sets the scene and comments on its significance, but retires from the picture when it is actually being taken so that his

La Terra Trema: 'Ntoni

presence is no longer felt. It ascribes to the director a role rather like that of the Cartesian God who winds up the clock and then allows it to run.

These logical difficulties are, however, largely indifferent to Visconti's purpose. It is perfectly possible to accept the film, as it is usually taken, as an effectively realistic account. But there is another parallel worth considering, which, in view of Visconti's later development, is of more immediate relevance, and that is the opera.[4]

In grand opera the words, and consequently much of the background to the action, are, because of the way they are sung, generally incomprehensible. What comes over from the stage are the elements of the action, the style of the setting, the grandeur and subtlety of the music. For a full understanding of what is going on, the spectator has to turn to the material supplied in the programme. A further feature of the genre, which has its origins in classicism

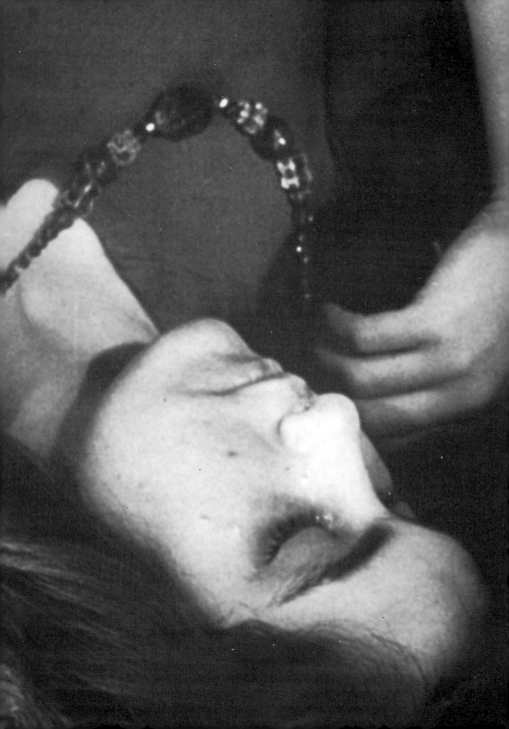

but survived well into the nineteenth century, is that the characters tend, for ease of recognition, to be stock types who owe their flesh and blood and their individual differentiation to the music and to their presentation on stage. Intentionally or not, *La Terra Trema* is an exact transposition of these procedures into the film medium.

I do not myself think that this can have been Visconti's original intention. The result is certainly paradoxical, but it also represents an extremely logical solution to the impasse in which Visconti found himself, and one that is in perfect conformity with his temperament and with his approach to the film, and the opera, as forms of spectacle. Not only the overall structure, but the detailed construction of each sequence is cast in an operatic mould. The action unfolds slowly, in a series of tableaux, with its choruses, solos and duets. The total effect is not realistic but lyrical. It is this need to present and to develop his material within a framework which, like that of opera, allows little weight to the dialogues and demands a completely different process of understanding from the normal novelistic or theatrical modes of exposition, that justifies the occasional *longueurs* and the faint aura of aesthetic indulgence with which the film is beset.

There are, then, three moments in the elaboration of *La Terra Trema*. The first, represented by the early scenario, is activist and would-be revolutionary. The second, marked by the return to Verga, shows Visconti in partial retreat from his intransigent position and submitting to a discipline of realism. In the third, having pushed this kind of realism to the point where it exploded in contradiction, he attempts to transcend it by imposing on the material a kind of lyrical exaltation through which he would be able to escape from the particularity of the second moment without falling back into the abstraction and tendentiousness of the first, and without doing violence to either the material or the ideological content of the film. The attempt fails, because violence *is* done. Visconti had got too enmeshed in the documentary morass to withdraw from it so neatly. He had got the people of Aci-Trezza to speak their own parts in their own way. He had accepted and even exploited the limitations of their appreciation of their own

53

situation. The method he chose to liberate himself from the impasse could not, however, transcend these limitations, it could only deny them, and at the same time deny or obfuscate the reality of the real lives with which he had involved himself.

The problem resolves itself as one of control. Visconti's method of presentation, which even in *Ossessione* is not entirely naturalistic and becomes progressively more stylised as time goes on, requires either an interaction between the actor creating the role and the director, or total control by the director of his material, including the actors, and of the effects to be drawn from it. In *La Terra Trema* this was impossible—or at best an illusory and deceptive possibility. The material was given, inflexible, and could therefore not be moulded into new expressive forms. This primacy of the material is often given as characteristic of the cinema as opposed to the theatre, and with *La Terra Trema* this is certainly the case. After making the film Visconti went back to the theatre, where he had already directed a number of productions ranging from Shakespeare to Cocteau and Tennessee Williams, and where, it seemed, he could exercise the control necessary to his artistic approach. But the dichotomy, as between cinema and theatre in the absolute, is unreal, and when, three years later Visconti returned to the cinema, it was to demonstrate its unreality, producing a work which was a supreme example of theatrical methods of control in making a film.

NOTES

1. In an even more indirect way *Senso*, Visconti's film about the Austrian occupation of Venice at the time of the *risorgimento*, appears to allude, by analogy, to the events of 1943–5. But the analogy is never explicit; see Chapter 5.
2. *L'Ecran français*, 7 June 1949, and Raymond Borde and André Bouissy, *Le néo-realisme italien*, Lausanne 1960.
3. *Bianco e Nero* 11, March 1951.
4. For a review of Visconti's opera productions see *Opera Magazine*, May 1958; and for a list of his work on the stage, and for the opera, see "Luchino Visconti" by Giuseppe Ferrara, *Cinéma d'Aujourd'hui*, no. 21.

3: Bellissima

It is unfortunate that Visconti's next film, *Bellissima* (1951), is not
better known outside Italy, as it is a film which, in addition to its
merits as an antidote to *La Terra Trema*, confounds a number of
stereotypes that have been built up round Visconti's work and
artistic personality. It is, in a vulgar sense, the most obviously
"Italian" of all his films, with extremely rapid dialogues which are
difficult to translate and *a fortiori* almost impossible to sub-title
without totally losing the flavour of the original. But it is the most
subtle and elusive thing of all, the element of self-criticism and
irony at the expense of its own "Italian" quality, which has most
effectively prevented it from being assimilated and appreciated by
foreign audiences. For at its highest level it is a denial of all stereotypes, about Visconti, about Italian films in general, about neo-
realism, and even about that sacred monster, Anna Magnani, who
is the star of the film.

The commonly held stereotypes about Visconti are that he is
totally humourless and incapable of self-irony, that his imagination
is sensual rather than intellectual, and that he is a crude social
realist with a taste for "positive heroes", and an anti-feminist who
neither likes nor understands his women characters. *Bellissima*
could at a pinch, by a spectator who shares these characteristics to
a rather greater degree than Visconti does himself, be read in these
terms. But it could equally well be taken in exactly the opposite
way. It is a comedy, highly verbal (not to say verbose), with a very

Bellissima: Maddalena Cecconi with Maria

simple and almost spare visual style; and its central character, presented and developed with great sympathy and understanding, is not only a woman but a woman visualised as an example of triumphant femininity. The only possible male candidate for the role of positive hero, or critical consciousness—the husband—is by contrast a colourless and insignificant figure. Social realism, as commonly understood, is also relegated to a minor role, subsumed under the general biting sarcasm with which Visconti tackles his background subject—the world of Cinecittà.

There is a danger, however, of asserting too strongly the extent to which *Bellissima* confounds the stereotypes. Take it too far, and a picture could emerge which was closer to Jane Austen's novels than to *Ossessione* or *Rocco and his Brothers*, and a very long way from Visconti. The trouble with the stereotypes is not that they are false, but that they are wrongly formulated—and therefore irrelevant. *Bellissima* is part of a highly coherent *œuvre*, and reflects the same artistic personality as the rest of Visconti's work, but it brings forward certain latent aspects of this personality and certain elements of a common structure of ideas which are less visible in some of the better known films, such as *Rocco and his Brothers*, and do tend to be overlooked. It is by overlooking these aspects and elements that external stereotypes have been imposed which bear little relation to the reality of Visconti's films. A close examination of *Bellissima*, and of the film of Visconti's it most resembles, *Il Lavoro* (his episode of *Boccaccio '70*) may help to break up some of the stereotypes and provide a more satisfactory impression of both the diversity and the underlying unity of his work.

Bellissima opens with a piece of apparently gratuitous *bravura*—a radio concert performance of a Donizetti opera. The camera prowls among the sopranos of the chorus, middle-aged dowdy maidens and matrons grotesquely miming the mood of an unseen romantic action. This suggestive reverie is brusquely interrupted by the intercutting of the brash voice of a radio announcer, giving details of a competition for "la più bella bambina di Roma"—"the prettiest child in Rome"—wanted for a star part in a new film. Given Visconti's well-known love of opera and the subsequent development of the satire on the world of Cinecittà, the contrast is clearly double-edged but on balance favourable to the old-fashioned world of the opera. As the unprepossessing ladies of the chorus mouth the word "bel-lis-si-ma" the image evoked is one of a misty ideal beauty, transcending the banal physical circumstances in which the image is produced—a sharp contrast between the product and the means of production which Visconti maintains in relation to the cinema throughout the film. Even the idea, however, of the "più bella bambina di Roma" exists only on the level of the most extreme vulgarity. It is a symptom of what Visconti sees categorically as a general cultural sickness of the contemporary Italian scene. Its only merit (and this is asserted in relation to pop music in *White Nights* and *Vaghe Stelle dell'Orsa*) is that it belongs unequivocally to the present, whereas opera is a fading glory of a more aristocratic, dying, tradition.

Much of the significance of this opening credits sequence is, however, only latent. Its immediate function is simply to establish a tone of gentle asperity, which is maintained, more or less evenly, throughout the film. The aspirant Shirley Temples and their mums swarm into the studios, with Anna Magnani, struggling wildly in the middle, looking frantically for her mislaid daughter. The errant infant is discovered playing quite happily by itself near an ornamental pool in the studio grounds, and when her mother approaches her and begins to fuss over her and scold her, there starts up a mad operatic duet between a screaming and shouting Magnani and a tearful, bawling child who does not understand in the least what any of the fuss is all about. Most of the humour of the film is centred round the themes announced in this episode, the different and conflicting forms of irrationality and non-rationality in the behaviour of the monstrous gaggle of middle-class mums, of Magnani herself, and of the little girl, Maria.

Unlike the other mothers, Anna Magnani is a "donna del popolo"—a "woman of the people". This "popolo" is not actually an invention of neo-realism as malicious critics have suggested. As a class, or non-class, comprehending broad strata of the population, it does exist, though more in literature than in real life.

58

Broadly speaking, it designates everyone who is not rich, bourgeois or upper class, whether shopkeepers, manual or white-collar workers, or nothing in particular. Some elements of a partly fictitious class stereotype, probably due to Zavattini, who wrote the script, have crept into the figuration of the character played by Magnani in *Bellissima*, but basically, largely because of Visconti's attention to untypical detail, the representation is autonomous and real and points a vivid but not implausible contrast between Magnani's character and that of the world to which the others belong.

Her husband is an amiable, commonsensical man, with a steady but ill-paid job and not many ambitions, least of all the extravagant wish that his child should become a national figure. Ambition, coupled with a slight naïve snobbery, becomes her province, and it is channelled through the child. With no particular illusions about her competence she calls herself a nurse, which means that she picks up money going round giving injections to hypochondriacs, of whom she knows a good many. Her vision of the world is dominated by the movies and by the ambitions she has for Maria. The role of the movies in this vision is providential, almost supernatural. They are not only a passion but a hope for miraculous advancement, either through fortune (like the lottery in Naples) or skill (like football in Rio). Magnani's slavery to the cinema dream and her superstitious hope have a background in popular life and help yet again to mark her off from the other mothers whose attitudes display a calculating bourgeois rationality. Times are changing, and what they have done is to transfer their ambitions from the middle-class world of theatre and ballet, to which they belong, on to a world which has the simple advantage of being quantitatively more lucrative, and which they mistakenly assume to be a part of their birthright.

The contrast between Magnani and the rest is reflected in their children. All the other little girls are theatrically trained or have been to ballet school and are precociously sophisticated and poised. In the end Maria emerges triumphant, despite her mother's last-minute attempts to train her and sophisticate her, precisely because she is not like the others. This is partly to be seen as a victory for

Bellissima: Maria at the dancing class

working-class spontaneity over bourgeois affectation (another probable contribution of Zavattini), but it also reflects a fact about the cinema, and the neo-realist cinema in particular. The little sophisticates are no use in front of the camera, where the child has only to look suitably childlike and the director and editor are supposed to take care of the rest.

Visconti, it seems to me, does not quite share this simplistic notion of screen acting which the story of *Bellissima* implies, either in theory or in practice. In fact, he is concerned to point to further areas of complication and contradiction beyond the question of spontaneity versus artifice. An important stage in Magnani's eventual disillusionment with the movie world is provided by an encounter with a girl in the cutting-room at the studio, herself a former star, chosen for a neo-realist film because she looked right for the part, and then dropped as abruptly as she was taken up. Visconti's criticism here does not stop short at the commercial cinema, nor is it simply moral and humane. Except in *La Terra Trema* he himself has always used professional actors, and, unlike for example Antonioni, he uses them for their professionalism. There is no doubt that he at least implies an aesthetic objection to the use of non-actors, and all the satire on irrelevant theatrical training should not be allowed to conceal an equal distrust of naturalness as an end in itself.

There is, therefore, a fairly explicit divergence between Visconti's attitudes and those of neo-realist populism. But the bulk of his satire remains reserved for commercialism and the parasitic apparatus of the movie industry, and for the contrast between Magnani's image of the cinema and the reality. This is a theme that has been treated by other Italian directors—notably by Fellini in *Lo Sceicco Bianco*[1] and by Antonioni in *La Signora senza Camelie*. But whereas Fellini and Antonioni were mostly concerned with sentimental and sexual alienation, Visconti misses out on this aspect altogether. There is no question of Magnani being corrupted by an ideal image of sentimental women's-magazine romance, to which she would in any case be safely immune. The film which she and her husband watch in the open-air theatre in the courtyard of their block of flats is not a sentimental melodrama but Howard Hawks's *Red River*, and her excitement at watching and recognising Monty Clift is the ordinary delight of any normal movie enthusiast. There is no particular significance either in the choice of sequence (the driving of the cattle through the river) except perhaps for a faint allegorical allusion to the herding of people which is a constant stylistic refrain in *Bellissima* itself.

What is criticised, therefore, is in the first place the heroine's uncritical and providential obsession with and belief in the cinema. There is no harm specifically in the film as a product: it is only when Magnani attempts to break into the process of production that she begins to pay for her obsession. She encounters a plausible young con-man who skins her for 50,000 lire on the grounds that he has influence, and then pushes his luck a bit by proposing a sexual rather than strictly commercial relationship. (The logic of this as simple prostitution does not escape her for one moment, even when she is most trusting and sympathetic to his advances.) Her next significant encounter, with the former star from the cutting-room, leads to her being admitted to the projection gallery when the results of her child's screen test are being shown. The test is an unmitigated disaster. The child is wooden, intimidated, uncomprehending; recites a poem in a sing-song voice and then collapses into typical floods of tears. The director's aides burst out laughing, with the kind of uncontrollable, inhuman laughter which recurs in many of Visconti's films. Only the director, Alessandro Blasetti,[2] played by Blasetti himself, remains, godlike, above the general hysteria, in divine (and equally inhuman) contrast to the bestiality of everyone else.

The final outcome is that Blasetti wants the child for the film, but by then Magnani has had enough. The results of the ambition which had first turned her head have now turned her stomach, and she renounces the proffered contract, reconciled to her patient and long-suffering husband and sanity restored.

It is difficult to take the ending entirely seriously. Neither the divine Blasetti (perhaps unconsciously modelled on Visconti himself) nor the ideally human Magnani, sentimentalised by Zavattini, nor even the ideal husband, carry much conviction. But following the general trajectory of the preceding plot the ending has complete internal coherence. That it does work, on its own level, is due partly to Visconti's sense of form and the particular stylisation he has imposed on characters and action, and partly to the conception of the central character and the way Magnani realises this conception. The only comparable example of this kind of imposed credibility, poising a vehement naturalism and spontaneity against a perfect stylisation, also involves Anna Magnani, and is Renoir's *La Carrosse d'Or*.

The aspects of stylisation and character conception are closely linked. Most of the people in the film move around in herds, a crowd of film people, of jabbering mothers, of women from the flats where Magnani lives. Their movements are conventionalised and stylised, almost those of slightly crazy automata, or of animals. Occasionally people move out of the herd to play as individual foils to Magnani, in the "duet" pattern characteristic of Visconti's films. Except in relation to her the stylisation allows of no element of conscious action or thought on the part of the characters. They "behave" rather than act. Magnani also "behaves". Her traditional star acting depends on a rapid exhibition of exaggerated behavioural responses. But underneath this surface exhibition she also thinks. She registers subliminally, summing up and suspecting the young man even when going along with him, preparing in advance for failure even when being most buoyant and aggressive. Her understanding and, following her understanding, her renunciation, mature slowly. Her intuition is always a step ahead, and her decision-making a step behind, her surface responses. Her completeness as a character emerges, not naturalistically, but through a kind of dialectical tension between naturalism and stylisation.

It is because of this method of presentation of her as a person that the humour extracted from her antics is never malicious. Nor is the humour surrounding the child. If Magnani is occasionally childlike in her apparent *naïveté*, the child in its turn is a miniature version of its mother, with occasional diabolical flashes of precocious wisdom. The child is a victim, but complaisant

Bellissima: Maria at the hairdresser's

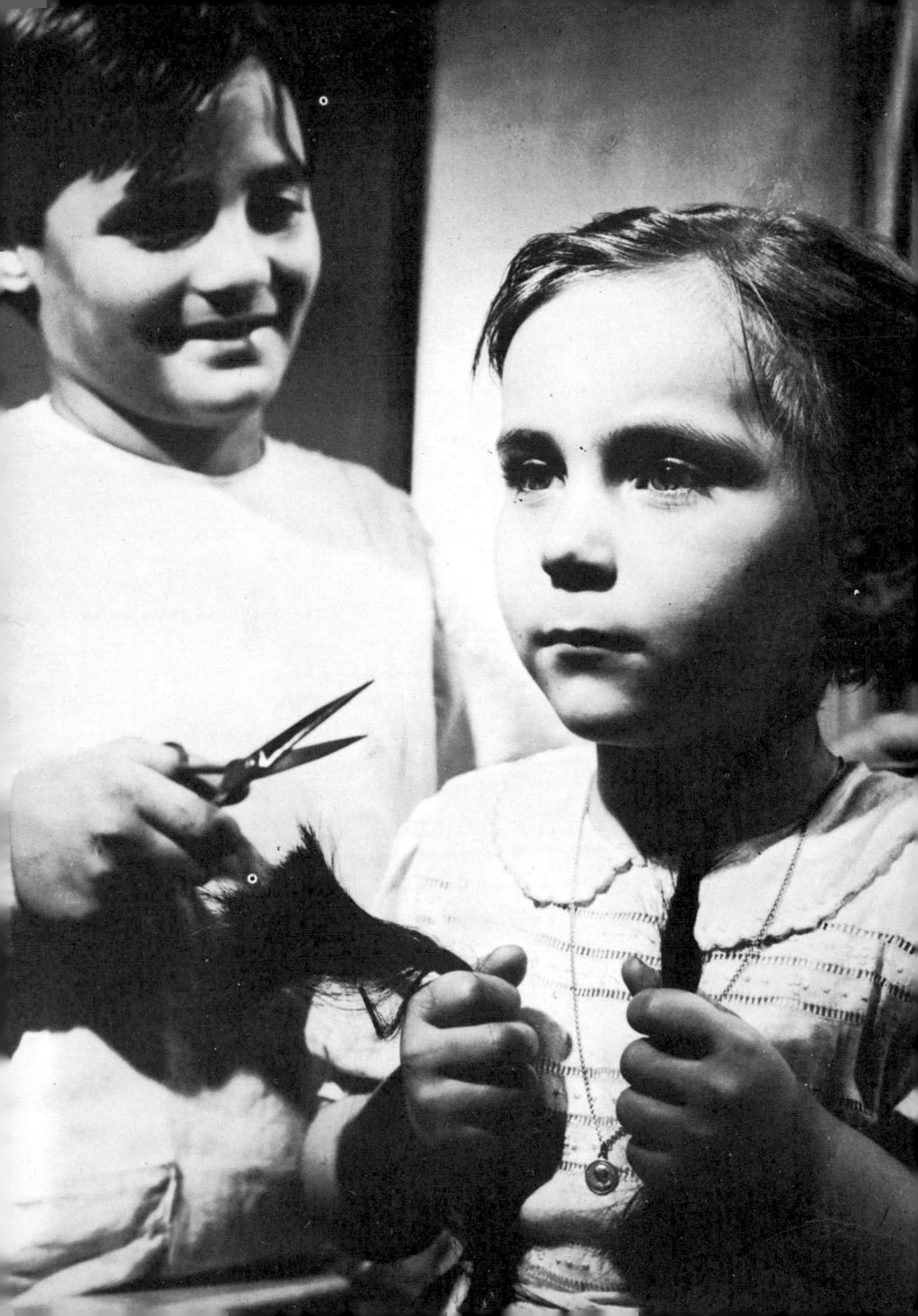

and impregnable. There is one particularly brilliant scene when Magnani leaves the child at the hairdresser's to be prepared for the competition. The job is entrusted to a diminutive girl apprentice, hardly much older than Maria herself. Instructed to trim Maria's plaits, she takes up the scissors tentatively, and then cuts off the plaits squarely near the top. Aghast, she turns for reassurance back into the shop; but the only eye she catches is that of Maria herself, who looks as if she is about to burst into one of her usual floods of tears, but then checks herself into a half-smile of complicity and delight.

In general the more a character emerges as an individual, the more sympathy is accorded them. Even the episodic figures like the absurd, parasitic, out-of-work actress who battens on Magnani and persuades her to let her give Maria some lessons in acting, are not seen as entirely grotesque. Comic hostility is reserved for the undifferentiated herd, particularly the mums. Real hostility, and not even comic, occurs only in the scenes involving the tycoons and parasites of the industry. It is here that a latent sense of violence and cruelty in Visconti's approach comes, rather uneasily, to light, together with a curious attitude to laughter as a manifestation, not of amusement, but of aggressive isolation.

Bernard Shaw once made an observation to the effect that extreme happiness produces tears, and extreme unhappiness laughter. With Visconti, tears are the product of extreme human emotion, and often, specifically, of deeply felt solidarity with someone else or of pity. Just once, with Natalia in *White Nights*, it is not pity but self-pity which provides the cause. Laughter, which occurs frequently in his films (the most quoted example is the laughter of Tancredi and Angelica at the dinner-table in *The Leopard*), is by contrast aggressive, always an expression of isolation, often of fear or hate. In *Ossessione* Gino laughs at Giovanna in the street to assert his independence from her and to cover up his own fears for himself. Franz, in *Senso*, does the same to Livia, while in *La Terra Trema* the wholesalers laugh at 'Ntoni in order further to humiliate him and so to gain their revenge for his insolence. Nadia in *Rocco and his Brothers* laughs desperately at

Simone, Romy Schneider hysterically at Tomas Milian in *Boccaccio '70*. Angelica's laughter in *The Leopard* covers up for a mixture of emotions—hate, jealousy, defensiveness, and a desire to shock. In *Bellissima* the laughter is pure cruelty. It has nothing to do with the gentle art of comedy, nor even with bitter sarcasm. It is the only moment in the film in which brutality breaks through to the surface.

Visconti would appear to have mixed feelings towards the phenomenon of hostile laughter. He uses it consistently, and to effect, but not always with a predetermined intention. The length and intensity of Angelica's and Tancredi's laughter appears to have been unforeseen before the actual shooting. He clearly regards it as a valid response, but also as indicative of suppressed hysterical violence in his characters, which ideally ought not to be there. Significantly, in *Bellissima* Blasetti does not laugh, but remains icy and calm. This may represent Visconti's picture of Blasetti, but I suspect that it contains at least elements of Visconti's picture of Visconti and that, to use a Freudian image, Blasetti is playing Super-ego to the Id of producers and technicians.

Either way we are faced once again with what seems like a false idealisation, but which can be justified. The morality of the artistic process is not that of life, and the cinema is an extreme case of this. There is a peculiar irony here. The brutal dropping of the girl in the cutting-room and the ignoring of Magnani by Blasetti are fair enough by one set of rules—those of artistic creation—but cruel by another. Visconti points this out, but to do so, in a film, he has himself been guilty of the same charge that he makes against the cinema in general because of the use he makes of the little girl Maria. There is then a second-degree moral attached to the main theme of the film. On the one hand he wishes to denounce: on the other he must himself carry through the very process that he condemns. Hence, if there is a touch of self-portrait in his presentation of Blasetti, that touch is critical, not only of Blasetti but of himself as well.

This point is, however, subsidiary to the main theme, which is a straightforward criticism of the cinema as an industrial and social process. The idealisation of the husband is essential here. Whereas in *Ossessione* and *Senso* there is a dynamic leading from husband to wife to lover to mistress, in *Bellissima* the lines of force lead in the opposite direction back to the husband, the only person with no connection with the movie world. Unlike Antonioni, whose films are fluid and open-ended, Visconti always relies on a rigid and self-contained structure. In *La Signora senza Camelie* the heroine at the end is left suspended, facing an uncertain but probably depressing future. Such an ending in Visconti's terms is inconceivable. Every story, which is a self-contained fiction, must have a determinate end. *Bellissima* is therefore constructed round a fixed point, which is the position of the husband. Both theme and structure require the figure to be overdrawn and to stand out clearly in the role, as for example the Spagnuolo did in *Ossessione*. The husband in this interpretation is neither a naturalistic figure nor a detached and abstract positive hero, but a concrete pole of attraction, holding the film together and allowing the clearest and most economical treatment of the central theme.

NOTES

1. *Lo Sceicco Bianco* is not strictly about the cinema, but about the far less glamorous world of the *fumetti*, photographic comic strips which are, however, because of their photographic realism, closer to the cinema than to comic strips proper.
2. Alessandro Blasetti, film critic and director, whose film *1860*, made in 1934, has been claimed as a "forerunner of neo-realism".

4: Il Lavoro

Up to this date Visconti's only other excursion into the field of screen comedy—or even semi-comedy—has been the sketch he directed for the episode film *Boccaccio '70* produced by Carlo Ponti and Antonio Cervi in 1962. As a film *Boccaccio '70* is ridiculous, but no more so than others of the genre. Intended, absurdly, as a kind of updated *Decameron*, it originally consisted of four sketches, each one hour long, by Fellini, De Sica, Visconti, and Mario Monicelli. But a four-hour film has to be a total blockbuster or it is nothing, and when it became clear that *Boccaccio '70* was not going to succeed on that level, Monicelli's sketch was removed from the commercially distributed version, leaving only the sketches by the three "great names". What survives is not so much a film as an anthology of mannerisms. The first episode, *Le Tentazioni del Dottor Antonio*, shows Fellini at his most masochistic: in the last, *La Riffa* (The Raffle), we have De Sica plumbing the lowest depths of synthetic populism: only the central episode, *Il Lavoro*, directed by Visconti, manages at all to avoid easy self-parody and to preserve some semblance of style and originality of content, and even there critics have had misgivings.

What Visconti does in *Il Lavoro* is to explore, with an uncharacteristically light touch, one or two variations on his favourite theme of class and sexual relations. A marriage is breaking up—for the very good reason that it never really existed. He is a young, charming, and indolent Italian aristocrat who keeps pedigree

Afghans and lives on the partly revived nostalgia of his bachelor days. She is the daughter of a wealthy German capitalist. She wears clothes by Chanel and her room is full of mewling white kittens. Their separate apartments in the *palazzo* are marked by contrasting décor. Her rooms are an island of opulent and sensuous feminity in the middle of an enormous building whose basic style was dictated by the classical and patriarchal taste of her husband's ancestors. Against this traditional but at the same time mildly bizarre setting they prepare to negotiate the future of their relationship. He surrounds himself with parasitic lawyers, and she takes advice over the phone from her father in Frankfurt. The result of these negotiations, conducted on both sides with great apparent seriousness, is a financial settlement. She decides that she can only preserve or acquire independence by taking a job. Lacking any skill or qualification other than sex, the only job she reckons she can do is prostitute herself. If he does not want her to do this actually on the streets or at the end of a telephone, then he must employ her himself, as he used to employ other women before and maybe still does. But the arrangement is to be back-dated, and he must start by paying her arrears for every time the couple have made love since they got married.

Most of the comedy of the film arises from the grotesque seriousness of the negotiations. Both the couple and their advisers act with an inhuman and humourless solemnity throughout. The proceedings acquire the air of a horrific, but plausible fantasy. But the seriousness of the protagonists should itself be taken seriously. They are not playing a logic game *à la* Lewis Carroll. It is not words but the frame of reference of their own actions that dictates the apparently absurd solution. With the aid of money and property she has physically constructed round her a world that is an extension of her as a person. She is living, childishly, in a private playground of her own creation. When she threatens to pack it all in for the sake of active independence in the world outside, she soon realises that her projected independence is in fact illusory. She is no longer insulated but is stripped down until she can be sure of nothing but her own physical existence not as subject but

Visconti on the set of *Il Lavoro*

as an object of use. She will exist only as a thing. The fact that her husband at that moment desires her physically as he might desire a prostitute makes the position desperately clear—but it also provides a way of escape. If sex is a commodity which men require and women can provide, she can at least impress on him her value as an object by demanding payment for her services. But since it is also clear that he married her partly for her father's money, which is not forthcoming, the roles are now reversed, to her advantage. Having first bought him, she is now charging him an economic rent as well.

The general critical reaction to *Il Lavoro*, at any rate in England, was that it was considerably less appalling than either the Fellini or the De Sica episodes of *Boccaccio '70*, and that it was Viscontian at least in style, even if the content was a bit thin and the Boccaccian joke rather long and drawn out. The thematic connection with Visconti's other films was on the whole neglected. But it is certainly there, and the relative success of the sketch is due to the fact that Visconti in *Il Lavoro* was drawing on themes and ideas common to many of his films and developing them in a concentrated and original way, without falling back, as the others had done, on self-parody and repetition.

In *Il Lavoro* Visconti takes up position against both his protagonists—against his insouciance and her petulance and vanity. But his main concern seems to be not to explore character but to demonstrate something about the situation. Sexual relations in Visconti's films do not ever exist in a pure state. They are always contaminated by other factors, such as violence, possessiveness, or (most frequently) money. Marriage is a particularly venal contract, but other forms of sexual relations are affected as well. Pure friendship can exist, but not a pure, sexually based love. Sexual relationships are by nature asymmetrical. Lovers have conflicting demands, very few of which are concerned with anything so simple as love or even sexual enjoyment. Generally speaking, men wish to use and women to possess. In bourgeois society (and all of Visconti's films, except *La Terra Trema*, are explicitly concerned with bourgeois society in one form or another) the desire to use or to

73

possess is inextricably connected with the power of money. In the absence of genuine and straightforward mutual love between equally matched partners, all forms of sexual relations can be reduced to two basic types: possession and prostitution. This reduction is expressed most clearly in *Ossessione* and in *Senso*, particularly the former, but it underlies even those films, like *Rocco and his Brothers*, which present sexual conflicts in a more complex form. In *Ossessione*, besides the relatively pure and uncontaminated friendship of Gino and the Spagnuolo, there are three main relationships: the marriage between the wealthy Bragana and the former semi-prostitute Giovanna; the possessive love of Giovanna for Gino; and Gino's casual liaison with Anita. Of these three it is only the last which is not in any way mercenary. Although the impression is fostered that Anita lives by exploiting such casual encounters, she gives herself freely to Gino. By a perverse and deliberate irony, what looks like a scene in which a man picks up a girl who seems willing to prostitute herself turns out to be the only one in which money is not involved. In *Senso*, however, the irony is suppressed. Clara, there, is bought by Franz, and the relationship is one of prostitution, with the marginal grace that the contract is at least open and straightforward and not hypocritical.

Class is a further complication. In *La Terra Trema*, where the relations between class, marriage, and property are set out with anthropological precision, not only is 'Ntoni's love for Nedda externally conditioned by their respective class situations, but it is psychologically inseparable from his other ambitions. There is, however, no question with Visconti of this being a peculiar sociological fact about "primitive" people which can be denied, in accordance with conventional schemas, when dealing with a more sophisticated society. In modern bourgeois society as well social pressures exist, and people are capable of internalising them in the same way. The specific difference is that in the primitive world of *La Terra Trema*, and also with the traditional aristocracy of *The Leopard*, sex and marriage are still seen as a form of cement, holding together the social fabric, whereas in the modern bourgeois environment they have been clearly reduced to commodities, both in fact and in the vision that people have of their own actions. Where a Visconti film introduces an aspect of class conflict in personal relations, it is always in conjunction with sex. Behind any individual complexities of character (and Visconti can hardly be accused of ignoring these complexities) the tensions created have their base in conflicting forms of sexual exploitation.

In this perspective the solution at the end of *Il Lavoro* is anything but absurd. The marriage of aristocrat and *bourgeoise*, without love or social necessity to support it, has simply revealed itself as an archetype of the two features—possession and prostitution—which Visconti sees as underlying sexual relations of any kind. In a sense a trick has been played on the audience to force them to see the situation in these terms. The situation at the beginning seems innocent enough, in everyday terms. A society couple is seen facing the usual problems of the break up of their marriage, reaching a financial settlement and trying to keep as much as possible out of the papers. All perfectly normal and unexceptionable—an inside view of an event details of which could be read between the lines of a newspaper gossip column any day. Then the picture changes. From the all too normal, expressed in the platitudinous surface naturalism of conventional marital drama, we move on to a different plane, that of the universal mechanism as Visconti understands it. The difference between *Il Lavoro* and Visconti's other films lies mainly in the fact that it is a comedy, and within the comic convention the mechanism, as a mechanism, can be more easily and even blatantly exposed.

This concern with laying bare the mechanism is unusual in Visconti's work. However clear an intellectual and structural vision he may have at the beginning of making a film, his involvement with his material and his recognition of human complexity often lead him by the end to render the vision opaque and even confused. Particularly in *Il Lavoro*, but also in *Bellissima*, he seems to be making an unaccustomed effort to ensure that the mechanical structure remains absolutely transparent and unambiguous. This is partly due to the fact that a spirit of comic detachment and even

of active hostility to his protagonists prevents any confusing and passionate involvement with the characters. At the same time, though, the mechanism is essential to the idea of comedy as practised by Visconti in his stage productions, and its appearance in the films is a direct reflection of his work in the theatre.

The film comedies occupy a position midway between the dramatic films and the classic comedies, from Shakespeare to Goldoni and Beaumarchais, which Visconti has directed for the stage. The procedure adopted by Visconti in theatre direction is, by all accounts, the inverse of that practised in the film comedies.[1] While the film comedies show a deliberate attempt to preserve clarity of texture, in the plays Visconti aims to give density and solidity to his re-creation of the text by the use of physical detail. The characters, often insubstantial as they step off the page, acquire consistency through their relationship with objects and background. The mechanism of the plays is brought down to earth and incarnated in physical reality.

These different procedures, applied to different material, in the end yield the same result. The style of presentation of the film comedies is extremely theatrical. *Il Lavoro* in particular is closer to a classic nineteenth-century French one-acter than to anything else Visconti has attempted in the movies—or than to Boccaccio for that matter. The action takes place in a confined set, while the privileged eye of the camera can explore with rather more freedom than can the spectator in the stalls. The meaning of the film is contained very largely in the dialogue, with only minimal help from action and gesture. The same is true, to a lesser extent, of *Bellissima*, where, even though much of the action takes place in the open air, there is still the same atmosphere of set-pieces theatrically presented and a similar virtuoso use of dialogue. Theatricality and comedy are presented as inseparable, both of them a kind of demi-reality amenable to detached and corrosive judgment from outside.

NOTE

1. See Roland Barthes, "Visconti et le Réalisme au Théâtre", in *Théâtre Populaire* 20, September 1956.

77

5: Senso

After *Bellissima*, with its happy matrimonial ending, Visconti turned his attention to the problem of divorce, a particularly contentious subject in Italy, where State law is the same as that of the Church—minus the casuistic loopholes. The Italian cinema has always been a focal point of controversy about the subject, witness the famous scandals of Roberto Rossellini and Ingrid Bergman and more recently Sophia Loren and Carlo Ponti. But it has always been more victim than aggressor. It has received publicity, most of it hostile, centred round the fact that Italian film people live according to a relatively permissive international ethos but are subject to repressive national laws. But it has never yet managed to go over on to the counter-attack and make its own propaganda by artistic means. Partly this is because its moral position is suspect—right-thinking opinion would never accept that a campaign in favour of divorce was suitably disinterested: partly, though, the reasons are political, as Visconti soon found out.

In the last few years one or two films have been made around the theme of Italy's archaic marriage laws. None of the films is very serious. A gentle satire of the worst absurdities of the situation (as in Germi's *Divorzio all'Italiana*) has proved a safe method of evading the vigilantes. In the early 1950s, however, the vigilantes of Church and State were on the attack. The project on which Visconti had been working was turned down by the nebulous but

79

none the less effective preventive censorship, and the film was never made.

Frustrated in his contemporary concerns, Visconti, with the active encouragement of his producers, turned his attention towards history. The producers' brief was for a "spectacle, but [sic] of a high artistic level"[1] and the precise story chosen by Visconti was a *novella* by Camillo Boito, entitled *Senso*. Like *Ossessione*, *Senso* was started as a result of the rejection of a more blatantly contentious subject, and, like *Ossessione*, it soon encountered censorship difficulties of its own. But again, even more perhaps than with *Ossessione*, we must avoid falling into the trap of seeing second choice as second best, resorted to exclusively as a result of censorship and production difficulties. Whatever the contingent factors affecting Visconti's decision, there is no doubt that his choice of a general subject—the Italian *risorgimento*—and even of that particular story of Boito, had more than accidental significance. Even if the choice were partly an accident, the accident itself was both significant and lucky. For *Senso* is beyond question one of the greatest, and also the most Viscontian, of all Visconti's films.

The choice of Boito's *novella* is, at first sight, surprising. The tone of the story is cool, neo-classic, and detached. The character of the Countess as revealed by the interior monologue is inconsistent and lacking in depth—possibly as a result of the moralism inherent in the tone. The observation of the background is superficial and uninteresting—again a result of Boito's uncertain attitude to his subject. But Visconti has usually preferred (*Bellissima* is an exception) to work from a literary original, however mediocre and apparently uncongenial. This procedure has the advantage of providing a firm point of departure, but he always claimed the right to maximum freedom in working towards the point of arrival. It is only recently, with *Il Gattopardo* and now *L'Etranger*, that he has accepted the discipline of literal and respectful adaptation of a major literary text.

By his own account[2] what first attracted Visconti to Boito's *novella* was the potential contained in the extreme situation of the story, rather than its actual content. The elaboration of the film went through several stages, each of which diverged further from the original and developed suggestions latent there but whose significance Boito had either not seen or interpreted differently. In the story the Countess, now middle aged, is seen looking back over a youthful aberration. The film shows her as already no longer young when the events took place, and (in what little remains of the rhetorical monologue) as still quite close to the events as she describes them. In the place of the frigid distancing of the story, Visconti makes it more immediate—and more anguished. But he adds a distancing of his own, partly by a stylistic trick at the beginning, relating his story to that of an opera, and partly by taking the story away from the Countess and setting it firmly in the external historical world.

The opening sequence, which is in itself a quite amazing *tour de force*, makes both of these points clearly. The titles come up against shots of a performance taking place at the La Fenice Theatre in Venice. After the final credit there is a title which reads "Venice, spring 1866. The last months of the Austrian occupation of the Veneto. The Italian government has made a pact of alliance with Prussia, and the war of liberation is imminent." As this title disappears Manrico launches into his famous aria "Di quella pira" and as that ends the camera pans to reveal the audience, first the Austrian officers in the stalls, then the crowds above and behind. There is a cut to the stage again, and then, as the chorus begins "All'armi, all'armi" ("To arms, to arms"), a cut back to the audience: one or two patriots moving to and fro; the furtive passing of objects from hand to hand. The music comes to an end. There is applause, formal from the military, enthusiastic from everyone else. Then a girl shouts out "Foreigners out of Venice!" and suddenly the theatre is full of rosettes and streamers in the Italian national colours. The colour effects are stupendous: the rich romantic browns of the stage set, the brightly coloured crowd in the balcony contrasting with the black evening dress of the *bourgeois* and the white uniforms of the officers in the stalls and boxes; then, finally, the red, white, and green streamers everywhere. In the uproar that ensues one hears shouts of "Viva La

Marmora" (leader of the national army) and "Viva Verdi!" (by coincidence the letters of the composer's name also spelt out the initials of "Vittorio Emmanuele, Re d'Italia"). The performance is suspended and gradually order is restored. The uproar dies down and the white uniforms and clipped Teutonic accents take over command.

It is against this background, which combines profusion and density of detail with extreme historical precision and clarity, that the personal drama is set off. In the general uproar that follows the demonstration an Austrian officer makes an insulting remark, and is instantly challenged to a duel by an Italian patriot. The patriot is the Marquis Roberto Ussoni, and the officer Lieutenant Franz Mahler. Ussoni's cousin, Countess Livia Serpieri, is watching the scene from the box where she is sitting with her husband and his friends, members of the Austrian High Command. In an effort partly to save Ussoni's life, partly to prevent him from exposing his identity (as an Underground leader he ought not to have allowed himself to be provoked and come out into the open), she asks to see Mahler. By this stage order is restored and the music has started again. Leonora's aria can be heard in the background. Livia is disarmed by Mahler's manner, a mixture of cynicism and military orthodoxy. But she manages, nervously and obliquely, to make her point, that the place for melodrama is the stage, not real life. Mahler is not to accept the challenge.

But this distinction between opera and real life is not intended to be maintained in a simple and rigid form. Already a parallelism has been established between the world of the audience and that of the stage. The style of the film is itself operatic, a pictorio-musical re-creation of a human drama. It differs from the opera in that the reduction to essentials is less complete. It is less "pure". The drama that is to be played out between Livia and Franz is a degenerate melodrama. In the true melodrama uncomfortable contingencies can be swept away; characters can become ideal. In the film, despite the lyrical exaltation, contingency and confusion of motive retain an essential role. Franz and Livia are being judged by the purer artistic standard of Leonora and Manrico as well as by the

83

standards of every day. It is more important to observe, from that standpoint, how far they fall short, than it is to niggle, from the standpoint of *petit-bourgeois* realism, at the way they seem unreally exalted above the social and psychological norm.

Franz does not fight a duel with Ussoni. Instead he denounces him—in conformity with his character and with military ethics. His conduct is not purely melodramatic. It is realistic, or degenerately melodramatic, according to the way you look at it. Livia meets him again, when Ussoni is being sent off into exile, and he follows her home, a white shadow (the word is his own) tracking her through the irreal Venetian streets along the canals. It is an accident —tripping over the body of a murdered soldier—that at the same time restores a sense of real historical context to the scene and brings Franz and Livia uneasily together. Later, when they fall in love, the differences in their situations and characters brought out in this short scene by the canals seem for a while to be submerged. But love conquers nothing. The contradictions are only exacerbated, and explode with greater violence for having been suppressed.

Livia and Franz make assignations at a boarding-house, and spend time together, fulfilling their respective dreams. Then Franz goes away. Livia waits for his return and one day, just as the Serpieris are planning to leave for their villa in the country, a message arrives with an address. Livia rushes out, pursued by her husband. He catches up with her outside the rendezvous, and she has just begun to confess when the door opens. But it is not Franz who had sent the message but Ussoni, who has secretly returned to Venice to raise money for the Partisans. Livia's consternation at not finding Franz is made worse by her guilt at having forgotten her loyalty to Ussoni and the Partisan cause, and by the embarrassment of her unnecessary confession. Fortunately Serpieri prefers not to believe her. His main concern is to make friends with his cousin Ussoni, whom previously he had repudiated. The political tide has turned against Austria, and the Count is swimming along with the tide.

The next episode brings Livia's conflicts to crisis point. Franz breaks into their country villa and she shelters him. She cradles his head in her arms as he sleeps, and her face seems to grow younger and fresher as the night goes on.[3] She wants him desperately, all the more so since she has become alienated from the Partisan cause. He wants her—but also what he can get from her, if necessary without her, which is money to corrupt a doctor to declare him unfit for service. He is not so much insincere as inconsistent, and a victim of external logic. Because he loves her and needed to see her he will be absent without leave. He could go one further and desert, but in that case will be shot if caught. With a medical certificate he will be in the clear, but will have to stay away from Livia and near his regiment in Verona.

Livia, partly out of fear for his safety, partly because she still hopes to hold him, gives him the money—out of the Partisan funds. Her betrayal is now total; but so is her sacrifice. The significance of her action is underscored heavily by the music and by long camera tracks along corridors; then more reflectively by the voice off. "I was now bound to him indissolubly. For him I had forgotten, betrayed, all those who in that moment were fighting, striving to realise dreams for which they had suffered so long." The scene is, to say the least, overwrought. What saves it from being, in the bad sense, melodrama, is the tragic futility of her gesture. The spectator is in a position of privilege. He is not invited to share her illusions, but to identify with the voice that comes, after the event, from behind the illusion, anticipating the end.

Against Franz's instructions, Livia follows him to Verona, and finds him, a drunken and guilt-ridden but lucid wreck, entertaining a prostitute. He drives Livia out, and she takes a final brutal revenge by denouncing him as a deserter. The Austrian general to whom she denounces him urges her to think again, rigidly loyal to the officer code. If denounced, Franz will have to be shot, but morally denunciation is the worse infamy. But Livia is not an officer and gentleman. The code is even more alien to her than it was at the beginning when she was trying to save Ussoni. Franz goes to the firing-squad, and the last shot of Livia shows her creeping away through the streets, calling his name, surrounded

by drunken soldiers celebrating a victory. It is almost as if she no longer existed. The indication in the script says "perhaps she has gone mad".[4] The story is left in suspense, and never reconnected with the hypothetical present tense of the voice off. Presumably Livia survives. But what she survives to or for is as irrelevant as the survival, after the tragedy, of Oedipus or Lear.

The personal drama, then, is self-contained. It ends with the death of Franz and the annihilation of Livia. But they are casualties of a wider process which does not end with their disappearance from the scene. At the end of the film the Austrians have just won at the Battle of Custoza, but on the world scale they are in retreat. They have already lost most of Northern Italy. They have lost to Prussia at Sadowa; and in the international political game this means that they will soon lose the Veneto as well. As the Austrian Empire declines, its place in the scheme of things is being taken by nascent bourgeois nationalism. The Italians, though defeated in battle, are in full self-assertion. "Sono una vera Italiana", Livia says proudly at the beginning, but at the end, having cut herself off from the nationalist current, she withdraws to the neutral and geographical "sono Veneta". Her destiny and that of Franz are not quite comparable. He is quite clearly seen as the representative of a dying class. She represents nothing so simple. Her character is all her own, and the conflicting external determinations that work on her are not sufficient to fix her in any mould. At least she has a freedom to abuse, which Franz never has.

At the same time, like Franz, she has her place in the wider picture. Married young, to an older man whom she doesn't love and whose interests she does not share, she takes up a position from the start against his cowardly time-serving. She becomes a nationalist, a political option which is also a move away from her husband towards her cousin, Roberto Ussoni. Her devotion to the cause is personal, and she betrays it because sexual passion has more power over her than devoted admiration and friendship. But her attraction to Franz has its own social motivation. Through it she realises a nostalgic longing for the lover to whom as a member of her class she was entitled, but never had. Against this patriotism

Senso: Livia gives Franz the money
Senso: Battle of Custoza →

has nothing to offer. In its first moment the *risorgimento* is too ideal. Later, as she comes to realise, it is not even that, but is the resurgence, under different colours, of craven *bourgeois* like her husband. It is not a cause which can fully satisfy her aspirations or appease her regrets.

Possibly the bitterest aspect of the background struggle is this resurgence of Serpieri, and its counterpart, the eclipse of Roberto. This is a theme whose significance, both historical and contemporary, could not fail to be clear to the aware Italian spectator, from the moment in which the scene is set by the historical title at the end of the credits. There is an implicit parallel between the events of 1866 and those of 1943–5. In each case, by a mysterious process of *trasformismo*,[5] the Italy which emerged from the upheaval was not substantially different from what it had been before. One *élite* replaced another, and the new *élite* came to look suspiciously similar to the old as the loyalists of the former régime came to reassume their positions under the new. More than a parallel however there is, here in *Senso*, a search for causes. The question that Visconti, as a Marxist, is asking himself is double. Did the revolution that might have happened in 1943–7 fail in the same way and for the same reasons as that of 1860–70? Or did it not also fail *because* the first one had failed, because the ruling class was allowed to establish a tradition of continuity, and *trasformismo* was allowed from the start to mask the conflicts that, objectively, seem to demand a revolutionary response?

Visconti does not produce a clear-cut answer. Nor does he force the parallel further than it can go. The lines along which he was thinking are suggested in a scene which unfortunately never saw the light of day but was cut out, so he claims, at the special request of the Ministry of the Armed Forces. In this scene Roberto, who is trying to bring in the irregular Partisan forces he has organised to outflank the Austrians at Custoza, is curtly informed by the Italian command that their services are not required. The army will win, or lose, alone. Roberto's reply is to the effect that if this is the victory, or defeat, the Italians want they can keep it. The substance of this scene is perfectly historical. The Venetian Partisans, like

Garibaldi himself, were a political embarrassment to the Cavour government, and like Garibaldi they were got out of the way. The final victory was therefore doubly remote from popular revolution. Not only did the Italian authorities reject the participation of the people: they didn't even score a victory for their own, limited cause. That was done for them by the Prussians at Sadowa.

Visconti's attitude to the myth of the *risorgimento* is therefore straightforwardly critical, and at times polemical. But the polemic does not interfere with the main burden of his analysis, which is concerned with the relationship of personal and class attitudes, rather than with political forces external to the main drama. If, for the purpose of analysis, one abstracts from the wider historical situation, the formal pattern which emerges is curiously similar to that of *Ossessione*. There is the same dynamic running through, from husband to wife to lover to mistress. Serpieri, Livia, Franz, and the prostitute Clara are doubles of Bragana, Giovanna, Gino, and Anita. There is also the same opposition between guilty passion and easy love as in the earlier film, and a similar pattern of impulse and betrayal. But behind these similarities there are also profound differences of form and content which reveal both a greater technical mastery and a vastly enriched vision of the world.

On the technical side there is, first of all, the use of colour. Visconti used three different photographers for *Senso*.[6] Each of these had a different approach to his work. It has been suggested, for example,[7] that if Aldo and not Krasker had shot the opening sequences in the Fenice Theatre the effect would have been very different. This is probably true, but it does not alter the fact that Krasker's lighting and shooting of the Fenice Theatre harmonises perfectly with Aldo's and Rotunno's work in other scenes. I would go further and say that Krasker's diffuse lighting gives absolutely the effect that Visconti needed for his opening sequence. Indeed, the use of different lighting effects, due to different photographers but co-ordinated by Visconti himself, is essential to the formal articulation of the film. Particular sequences and locations each have a tonality of their own, inspired often by different styles and genres of nineteenth-century painting. Venice by day is pastel and insubstantial, like a watercolour, except for the Serpieri *palazzo* with its sombre academic interior. By night it has a tonality which is prevailingly blue. This might be an accident, due to the difficulties in rendering the colour, but the same tonality is present in the shots of Verona at the end when Franz is shot, and the association of that final scene with the scene by the canals is surely deliberate. The move from the *palazzo* in Venice to the country villa is marked, naturalistically enough, but expressively as well by a sudden brightness with lots of brilliant green, and the same deceptively simple effect is continued for the battle scene. The soldiers seem at first like the figures in old military prints, then the picture darkens, almost to Goya. The ideal image gives way to gruesome reality.

Besides giving an expressive tonality to particular scenes the colour also serves to delineate the formal components of the film: the places—Venice, Verona, the country retreat: people—Livia's fleshy sensuality and the superficial picture of Franz as a "chevalier sans peur et sans reproche"; groupings, even emotions. *Senso* has a formal clarity which *Ossessione*, for all its apparent simplicity, does not achieve. This is due to the contrasts, at every level—form as well as content—between its various interrelated parts. The private and public dramas interlock. The characters move, at first blindly, with the general historical momentum or according to traditional paths, and are then shocked into consciousness when they find that the two conflict, either with each other or with some other half-conscious choice. The tension and the tragedy arise from their realisation that they are, or have become, something that the world does not allow them to be.

The world which the characters inhabit is dense, orderly, and on the verge of collapse. Besides the pictorial and temporal construction already analysed, it has a complex and tightly-knit social structure, whose elements are first displayed in the opening sequence at the theatre. Each pictorial block brings to the fore a particular element or grouping, and Livia's progress is charted in terms of the structure, which underlies and limits her freedom of action. She rebels against its limits, but cannot break them. She

Senso: Livia

starts from a position at the centre, comfortably but insecurely related to all groups in the action—to the Austrian command, the collaborators, the patriots. Then, as her affair with Franz first gains and then loses its momentum, she gradually moves away towards total isolation, estranged from her husband, evasive to the patriots, in conflict with every code, including finally that of Franz himself. The only contact she preserves until near the end is Laura, her maid and confidante, who has the role of mediator between her extravagances and the ordered world outside. But Laura's protection and complicity in hiding her affair from her husband give her a false sense of security. They just make it easier for her not to be fully aware of where she stands.

Although it is Livia who occupies the centre of the stage, in social and historical terms it is Franz who is the more interesting character. It is Franz whom Visconti locates most precisely in his situation, and having defined the situation creates, almost from nothing, out of the faceless cipher Remigio Ruz of Boito's original, the most fascinating individual figuration in all his work. Franz is a romantic of the second generation. His favourite poet is Heine, but a Heine whose irony has been transmuted into something approaching total cynicism. Not that Franz himself is exclusively cynical. But his romantic dreams of love and of a world without nationalism and national frontiers are too remote from the role in which he has been cast. Not only are they unsustainable in real life, but they contain all too obvious elements of self-deceit. A tirade against nationalism comes hypocritically from the lips of an agent of imperialist repression. Franz believes in what he says; but his belief is a mixture of irrelevant idealism and distaste for his job. He chose to be a soldier because he thought it was a game—an extension of childhood with drink and women thrown in as extras. The reality of war horrifies him. Hence both his horror of nationalism and his wish to desert. His feelings about romantic love are strictly analogous to his feelings about soldiering and war, except that he affronts the prospect of being a great lover with slightly less *naïveté* and rather more enthusiasm. But even here he is torn between conflicting ideals. Livia destroys him, involuntarily, long before the moment when she betrays him to the authorities, by occupying his area of freedom. She makes demands on him which he cannot satisfy, and the time comes when he finds himself trapped. He is no longer an adequate soldier and a competent Don Juan, but a potential deserter and a miscast and unwilling Romeo. Given what, in Livia's eyes, would be a straight choice between the army and her, he hesitates. Unlike her he has no desire to sacrifice anybody or anything, least of all himself. He plays to have it both ways: sees her, takes the money, and escapes. But whereas she remains buoyed up by a romantic illusion, or rather by a knowledge that she has made her choices and can stick by them, he is completely broken. Despite his lack of patriotic idealism his life was totally bound to the army and the army code. Having deserted—in fact if not in law—not only does he feel guilt at what he has done, but he finds himself an outcast. The whole fabric of his life collapses around him. The army had told him who he was and prescribed limits for him—times when he could make love or get drunk, thoughts he could think and things he could or couldn't do.

The final blow to his freedom and self-respect is that he has been deprived of his masculine right of initiative. He has become a kept man. The role of money in sexual relations is a favourite theme of Visconti's, whether it is the custom of the dowry (as in *La Terra Trema*) or the clash between aristocratic and bourgeois ideals (as in *Il Lavoro*). There is a close parallel between Franz and Gino in *Ossessione*. It is when Gino learns about the insurance, and realises that from now on he will be tied to Giovanna's *petit-bourgeois* apron-strings, that he feels the hand at his throat and makes his half-hearted gesture of defiance. Franz is less half-hearted. Quite consciously he elects to keep Clara on the money given him by Livia, and also to conduct his relationship with her in such a way as to make it quite clear, this time, when nothing else is left, who is in command. But it is only when Livia rushes in, unwanted and unannounced, that these ideas are forced to the surface. He uses them with the express purpose of avenging himself on Livia, and it doesn't really matter to know how explicitly conscious he was of what he was doing before she arrives. With the submissive and

innocent Clara he had found some peace and compensation for his other losses, and Livia's arrival is not only an embarrassment: it is a brutal reminder of all his shame and guilt. Stirred into consciousness, he sets about purposefully humiliating her, taunting her with her age and ugliness as well as with corruption and cowardice.

But there is more to Franz's tirade than a cruel and disabused denunciation of their love-affair. Motivating his apparent disgust there is a clear and far less moralistic awareness of belonging to a dying race. The Austrian victory at Custoza is meaningless. Austria is in decline, and with the Austrian Empire a whole class and a whole world will disappear—that to which Franz belongs, and so does Livia. Hence Franz's bitter pride in having denounced Ussoni, whom he sees as representing the new world to which he will never belong.

Franz dies lucidly, but not passively. He does not allow himself the stoic luxury of a dignified death, but shouts and struggles right to the moment when he is shoved up against a wall and shot. His life was all he had, and like Heine he revolts against the idea of death—"O Gott, wie hässlich bitter ist das Sterben." To the last he remains consistent, an embittered romantic of a generation on which Byronism had turned sour. To be precise he is, in the full sense of the word, a decadent; and it is as a study of decadence that *Senso* carries its most complete and perfect conviction.

Although in terms of structure and plot Franz is like a reincarnation or perhaps a prior incarnation of the Gino of *Ossessione*, the themes which he introduces are new, a sign of Visconti's liberation from the "progressist" schemas of neo-realism. In his lucid self-consciousness he had a forerunner, of a kind, in the figure of 'Ntoni in *La Terra Trema*, but unlike 'Ntoni's his consciousness is completely negative and backward-looking. In all of Visconti's films, including the first, the past is seen as a burden, but while in *Ossessione* and *La Terra Trema* the characters can at least see the burden as outside themselves, something that can and must be shaken off, from *Senso* onwards the burden is more like a hump, something ingrown from which there can be no release. Only the progressive but pallid Ciro, in *Rocco and his Brothers*, seems

Senso: Franz and Livia

capable like 'Ntoni of rejecting the past. The other characters are
forced to bear with it, complacently or despairingly, to the end.
The much-abused label of "decadent" which has been attached
not only to the characters but to Visconti himself, is meaningful
only in these terms. Visconti's approach is not indulgent: even in
his treatment of the incest theme in *Vaghe Stelle dell'Orsa* there is
little of the morbid fascination of full-blown D'Annunzian decadentism. Nor is it moralistic. The moral degeneration and moral
incapacity, which are features of the world described in Visconti's
films from *Senso* to *Vaghe Stelle dell'Orsa*, are to be understood
first of all historically, as products of a response to a historical and
class situation in which the individual feels himself bound by the
past and unable to adapt to the present.

On the other hand I would not wish to maintain that Visconti's
approach is totally analytic and detached. He is involved with his
material, and has a personal stake in what he is saying. As an
aristocrat who has thrown in his lot with a cause which ultimately

implies his own destruction and that of his class, his focus of interest is quite naturally (though not inevitably) the points at which the theoretical analysis which he accepts encounters his own personal situation. In *Senso* this focus is in fact double—the "decadence" of Franz and the stumbling and erratic "progress" of the world around. It is this antithesis of progress and decadence which has been particularly misunderstood and fetishised by Visconti's critics. We shall return to it later. At this stage it seems best to carry the narrative forward to *The Leopard*, a film in which the historical themes of *Senso* are taken up again and treated, perhaps with less brilliance, but with a subtler awareness of the issues; in which, also, the double focus of *Senso* is fused into one.

NOTES

1. Quoted in *Luchino Visconti: Senso* in the collection *Dal Soggetto al Film* published by Cappelli.
2. *Visconti: Senso*, cited above.
3. Characteristically, the ghouls of naturalism find this scene particularly offensive and ridiculous, as they would doubtless find the obvious parallel with the Michelangelo *Pietà* in St. Peter's, in which the Virgin is shown as actually younger than the Christ whose body she is holding in her arms.
4. *Visconti: Senso*, cited above.
5. *Trasformismo*, in Italian history, is the name given to the process whereby seemingly dangerous elements were "transformed" into stable parts of the system. As a political tactic it is particularly associated with Giolitti, Prime Minister around the beginning of the century.
6. G. R. Aldo, Robert Krasker, and Giuseppe Rotunno. For details of which scene was shot by which, see Filmography.
7. *Visconti: Senso*, cited above, p. 212.

6: The Leopard

Franz's vision of events at the end of *Senso* had one blind spot. He identified as his enemy Ussoni, the man to whom Livia could have a pure loyalty and who was an incarnation of the new order. But objectively Ussoni failed. An aristocrat who had freely crossed the barrier to the other side, he was to learn that the new order was in fact the property of the abject Serpieri. The new order was to be just like the old, without the glamour and the graces and with the bourgeoisie playing a more autonomous role. Part of Franz's bitterness was therefore misplaced.

In *The Leopard* the romantic extremes of *risorgimento* idealism and post-Byronic cynicism, represented in *Senso* by Ussoni and by Franz, are replaced by a far less dramatic conception. *Trasformismo*[1] is the order of the day. The bourgeoisie marry into the aristocracy and the Byronic aristocrat sinks gently into *bien-pensant* mediocrity as the revolutionary storm subsides. The pessimism of *The Leopard* is no less absolute for being less extreme than that of *Senso*. It is subtler, more delicately shaded, but its final effect is even more gloomy. There is no contradiction of forces, just a gradual decline of old and new alike, supervised by an ageing and melancholy patriarch.

Visconti's interest in the central theme of Lampedusa's novel—the gradual submergence and transformation of an aristocratic Sicilian family at the time of the *risorgimento*—was in a sense predictable. But that he should be prepared to make the film, in

The Leopard: Don Ciccio

association with Twentieth Century-Fox, as a multi-million-dollar spectacle was disquieting, both to the proprietorial lovers of the original novel and to the nostalgics of neo-realism. Their fears were not entirely baseless, but not quite for the reasons they put forward. If *The Leopard*, as finally realised, is not altogether a satisfactory film it is not because it crudifies, in translation on to the large screen, the intimate novelistic concerns of Lampedusa. Visconti was not fool enough to attempt such a translation. He re-created the story in his own terms, taking full advantage of all the possibilities of modern techniques. He made no attempt to render certain subtleties which were peculiar to Lampedusa's narrative style, but this does not mean that his own conception was crude. He rejected intimacy as both technically and ideologically inappropriate but used the large Technirama screen and the latest Technicolor process to give a profusion and richness of detail which the small screen and black and white could never achieve.

Unfortunately, despite his many previous chastening experiences with Italian producers, Visconti did not reckon with the extraordinary philistinism of Twentieth Century-Fox. They, for reasons entirely of their own, decided to distribute *The Leopard* in England and America only in a mangled and pathetic version. It was scaled down from seventy millimetre to thirty-five millimetre, printed on inferior colour stock, and shorn of some of the most important scenes. As if this were not enough it was then post-synchronised with an insensitivity which it is often hard to credit, particularly if one bears in mind the relative skill with which low-budget spectaculars by Freda and Cottafavi are dubbed for the English market. Visconti himself had no control whatever over the dubbing, which was supervised by Burt Lancaster. Possibly, however, listening to Lancaster speaking his lines in English on the set, he may have had some vague premonition of what the English version was going to be like. In that version Lancaster dubs himself, sounding for all the world more like a gruff Western patriarch than a Sicilian prince. The final ballroom sequence, with the continental actors dubbed into a variety of mid- and transatlantic accents, is an indefinable mixture of the ball in *The Big Country* and a fancy-dress party in a small town in the Mid-West. The dialogues too have suffered from translation. In the finale in particular they have acquired an utterly inapposite vulgarity and flatness which, if nothing else, is in blatant contradiction with the suggestivity and carefully created period atmosphere of the original script and of the sets. It is small wonder therefore that Visconti has repudiated the English version of *The Leopard* and accepts no responsibility for it at all.

All this makes it very hard, for someone who has not seen the original, to reach a balanced assessment of the film which Visconti intended and actually realised. Not having seen it myself I shall limit my comments to those aspects of the film which do emerge successfully from the American version, correlated by references to the original script,[2] hazarding the occasional guess about those other aspects which were presumably intended to emerge but unfortunately do not.

Lampedusa's novel was an almost mystical account of the unchanging essence of Sicily and what was for him its most representative class, the landowning aristocracy. It was a story of lethargy and inertia, seen as natural products of the sun and the earth, mysteriously preventing change. At the same time it was an elegy for human mortality. Sicily seems to inspire mystical reflection of this kind, even in its realists. There is a trace of it in the fatalism of Verga, and more than a trace in writers who, like D. H. Lawrence, came to the island from the outside. Shorn of its mystifying elements, the basic image is quite close to reality. For two hundred years or more Sicily has been stagnant economically, the despair of well-meaning politicians, festering in isolation under the wasteful exploitation of its natural resources. It is at the same time extremely beautiful.

As *La Terra Trema* showed, Visconti's attitude is far less indulgent than that of literary tradition towards the "poetry" of the island. While Lawrence could use Sicily as a staging-post on his spiritual pilgrimage towards the deeper mysteries of Mexico, Visconti (like Eisenstein in Mexico) is only partly responsive to the

mysterious character of Sicilian history and life. Where Visconti keeps most closely to the picture created by Lampedusa is in his reliance on sensual evocation and his interest in the central theme of the novel, the self-interrogation of an aristocrat obsessed with the need to account for his own survival. But the film differs from the novel in the explanations it puts forward of why the Sicilian aristocracy (of which Lampedusa was a member) survived. Visconti's explanations are to be found in history, which appears, not, as in the novel, in the form of the rumblings of a distant storm, but as a protagonist. The House of Salina, in the film, is directly involved in the process of transformation. It is political and economic cunning which enables it to survive, not a magic spell cast on the island to protect it from change.

Compared with *Senso*, perhaps, Visconti's *Leopard* does appear to make concessions towards the viewpoint of the text from which it is adapted. But it would be more accurate to describe them not as concessions to Lampedusa, but as changes in Visconti's own approach. Even more than in *Senso* he is concerned with the process whereby revolution became transformation and transformation *trasformismo*. The private dramas are not allowed to run, as they did in *Senso*, in contrary directions: they are subordinated to the main development. At the opening of the film the world is polarised into Borbonici and Garibaldini. The House of Salina is threatened with expropriation. Tancredi, the Prince's nephew, to the consternation of all his family except his uncle, goes off to join the revolutionaries—thus associating the family conveniently with the winning side. Gradually the revolutionary *élan* of the Garibaldini gets swallowed up. Tancredi becomes an officer in the Piedmontese army. Gradually too the Salina household comes to terms with the new order and *vice versa*. The Prince votes in the plebiscite for unification with the North. Tancredi marries the daughter of a *bourgeois* and she and her father are drawn inexorably into the old world. In the ball at the end of the film, given by another of the surviving aristocratic families, a boring old colonel repeats until even the Prince is nauseated by it the story of how he saved the new monarchy by shooting Garibaldi at

Aspramonte. The forces of the new reaction are now solidly entrenched.

In the process, however, the Prince has grown old. Though he has done his utmost to protect his family from destruction and to adapt to changes in the order of things, he sees no role for himself in the new scheme. He rejects a request, brought by a Piedmontese emissary, that he should take a seat in the new Senate. If there is to be a new order, he maintains, it should be new, and he cannot take part in it. He has resigned himself to events, but cannot desire them or look on them with satisfaction. Even in regard to his family he has failed. The price of protection for his daughters has been decadence. These nervous immature maidens, brought up in the close atmosphere of an isolated aristocratic household, are incapable of taking their place in the world outside. For Tancredi the price of adaptation has been betrayal. He is not decadent: he is all too accommodating. After his first impulsive decision to join the Garibaldini, which is a betrayal of most of what his family stands for but is also a positive revolutionary commitment, he then retreats step by step, abandons the red shirt of the Garibaldini for the blue uniform of a career officer with the Piedmontese, and gradually assumes a more and more conservative stance which reflects itself not only in his ideas but in his manner, his clothes, even in his face.

Tancredi's increasing sobriety in everything else is balanced by a growing possessiveness towards Angelica. Her family is bourgeois, her father, Don Calogero Sedara, is shown as an uncouth plebeian snob, rising rapidly on the historical tide, whilst being subjected to a defensive and uneasy ridicule by the aristocratic "Leopards". She herself, as played by Claudia Cardinale, has an earthy, if frigid, beauty and a physical vigour which is carefully contrasted with the anaemic inbred appearance of Tancredi's cousin Concetta. Tancredi's preference for Angelica over his cousin has, therefore, both class and sexual bases which are inseparable from each other. The old aristocracy has reached the end of the line. Angelica's beauty and vitality are class characteristics as well as individual, and by following his natural sexual inclinations Tancredi is also challenging the social order—more radically perhaps than he did by opting for Garibaldi against the Bourbons. For a moment, indeed, it looks as if this will happen. Concetta's ill-masked distress, Sedara's gaucheness, Angelica's violent and ill-judged laughter at a faintly risqué joke of Tancredi's greeted with stony silence by the rest of the company, all threaten a complete rupture of family relations. It also seems, particularly in the scenes where the lovers wander together round the echoing attics of the palace of Donnafugata, as if Tancredi's love for Angelica will take him not only away from his family but out of himself, that passion will be stronger than social pressure. But the kind of conflict which most often exalts and then destroys characters like Gino, Livia, Simone, or even Gianni[3] never fully develops. The forces are unequally matched. The House of Salina adapts and absorbs the couple, and leaves them the prospect, which they happily accept, of easy conformity in the context of a very typical marriage.

The final ballroom sequences, which seemed to the American producers of no narrative significance and therefore open to drastic reduction and mutilation, bring together the mind and memory of the Prince. The importance of this subjective aspect appears to have been lost on the producers and their technical henchmen, and the scene, in the English version, has lost all its internal coherence. Visconti's intention was to reproduce cinematically and pictorially the content of what in the novel was a long interior monologue by the Prince, his reflections on change and recurrence, and on life and death. The Prince wanders from room to room, watching the scene, and participating in it fully at one moment only, when he is prevailed upon to dance a waltz with Angelica. As he walks round he sees things which reminded him of his past life and of the fact that he is now old. Women who have been his mistresses are now aged and stately dowagers. A new generation has succeeded his, that of Tancredi and Angelica on the one hand and his own daughters on the other. When he accepts to dance with Angelica there is a double poignancy in his response to her request. Her naïve flattery serves as yet another reminder of the difference in age between them. But at the same time there is something provocative about

The Leopard: Angelica dancing with Don Fabrizio

her insistence which makes him realise that he is still young enough to desire her, even acutely.

This episode follows directly, and by subtle contrast, a morbid scene in which his eye is caught by a monstrous academic painting of a death scene, and he shocks Tancredi by the vivid realism of his observation about the cleanness of the sheets. There is no interior monologue, and the dialogues are brief, sardonic, and allusive. The meaning is conveyed, not just by the words but by a permanent relationship which is set up between the Prince and what he sees around him. The misty colour effects, the choice of detail, the cutting and camera movement[4] gradually and unobtrusively build up a kind of dialogue between the man and his surroundings. There is no visual or rhetorical expressionism. Everything is real, but seen in a particular way, refracted through the consciousness of the Prince. Stylistically it is the perfect cinematic equivalent of Flaubert's *style indirect libre*.

A lot of what should be present is lost in the English version, as a result of cuts, dubbing, and shoddy printing, but enough remains for Visconti's stylistic mastery to assert itself in the most resounding and unequivocal fashion. Where doubts arise is not over this achievement but over the actual matter of what Visconti is saying. Not for the first time, he seems to have let himself be seduced by an aspect of his subject which revealed itself during the elaboration and shooting of the film and to have developed that aspect at the expense of others. The obvious parallel is with *Rocco and his Brothers* (see below, Chapter 9). In *The Leopard* the pomp and splendour of the aristocratic ball and the patriarchal figure of Burt Lancaster as the Prince appear almost to have taken precedence over the themes developed earlier in the film, and gradually edged them out to allow for the virtual transfiguration of the Sicilian aristocracy in the tremendous finale. Not only has the episode grown in physical size, so that contrary to original indications it now lasts, in its complete form, for well over an hour. It has also acquired a character of unquestioning nostalgia. Where the film had previously taken a critical attitude to the events described, it now slides gently into sharing the point of view of one of the

On the set of *The Leopard:* Visconti with Burt Lancaster

protagonists. Given the manner in which the Prince has been
idealised as a figure right from the beginning, the move into
indirect libre can be interpreted only in one way, as identification
by Visconti with the central figure.

The closing images of the film, however, are ambiguous. The
Prince takes leave of the company to walk home alone. The streets
are very quiet in the clear autumnal dawn. The silence is broken by
a clattering of bells as a priest walks past with two young acolytes
on his way to early Mass. An organ-grinder strikes up. The Prince
walks away and in the restored silence stops to mutter a semi-
religious invocation to the morning star. Then the silence is broken
again, abruptly, by a brief volley of gunfire. Some rebels are being
shot. The sound of the guns re-echoes through the streets, as the
rest of the family return in their coach. The Prince goes on
walking towards the sea.

To a certain extent the ending retrieves the film from the aura of uncritical nostalgia into which it had been immersed. It takes it out of the close atmosphere of the *palazzo*, away from the splendour and solidarity of the gathering of aristocratic clans. Death is a solitary thing, whether for the Prince or for the rebels. The Prince does not articulate his feelings when he hears the shots, and the juxtaposition has to speak for itself. But besides the general reflection on mortality there is also present a harsher, more critical comment—on the price of survival. The Prince can afford to choose the moment when he feels he wants to die. Not so the rebels. The transformation of the House of Salina is the rebels' defeat.

But even attributing this significance to the closing moments of *The Leopard* does not resolve the ambiguities with which the film is beset. In the two *risorgimento* films and in *La Terra Trema*, Visconti has given three accounts in all of the failure of attempted revolution and the continued dominance of the old order. In the first, *La Terra Trema*, he takes the point of view of the exploited fishermen, and his explanations are straightforwardly economic and political. The fishermen neither have the political organisation and economic power to overthrow their oppressors; nor, being attached to private property as a means of advancement, do they understand the need for collective action and organisation. They fail, and Visconti's heart is with them in their defeat.

In *Senso*, however, the division of the world into oppressors and oppressed is less clearly marked. The categories are political and ideological rather than economic, and the action takes place between groups and individuals whose functions are not determined exclusively by economic factors. The way the forces are aligned and the way in which individuals become representative not only of groups but of ideas shows clear traces of the influence of the sophisticated theories of Gramsci on Visconti's previous rather crude conception of the class struggle. The artistic structure of the film removes it still further from the level of a historiographical textbook. The forces in play are basically those of progress (Ussoni), decadence (Franz), and conformity and *trasformismo* (Serpieri), and the motor of the action on both individual and social planes is betrayal.

The Leopard: the Prince studying astronomy

Visconti's own position is detached. The film is seen through the eyes of Livia, who chooses, betrays her choice, and is herself betrayed, but it does not identify itself with her.

In *The Leopard*, finally, the causes of failure are seen as absorption and adaptation. As an explanation this is as valid as the others, but the way in which it is put forward is distinctly ambiguous. Whereas in *Senso* Visconti retains a position of detachment above a central character who is directly involved in the action, in *The Leopard* Visconti's position is apparently one of identification with a central character who is himself as detached as is humanly possible from the events that are taking place. The Prince's great passion is astronomy, and his view of life is accordingly distant and macrocosmic. At no point does he participate directly in the action, except briefly when he accepts to dance with Angelica. Everything is seen *sub specie aeternitatis*. Even the dance is only an enactment on human scale of the eternal gyration of the stars. Identification with such a superhuman viewpoint effectively denies any involvement at all.[5]

The problem with the Prince is that although he is subjectively above the action and is symbolically represented as having that role, he remains a member of a particular class: his consciousness is class-bound consciousness, and his actions form part of the class action of the aristocracy to which he belongs. "We are the Leopards," he says at one point, "and the others will always envy us." This remark, like others in which this patriarchal figure comments on things related to his family, is particularly ambiguous, because it poses the problem of detachment and identification at so many different levels.

We can perhaps resolve these difficulties most simply in this way. The position which Visconti takes up in *The Leopard* in the face of historical change is equivocal. He rejects both the simple "leftist" solution of seeing it from the point of view of the Garibaldini and their successors, and the liberal compromise of balancing abstractly two points of view. At the same time he stops short of complete identification with the old order. He is telling the history of the aristocracy from the inside through one of its representatives, but he dissociates himself from the story in two ways. In the first place the character who concretely personifies the historical movement is himself detached, and Visconti identifies with him in his detachment. But because he is also class-bound, through his involvement with his family, a further act of withdrawal is necessary at the very end. The shooting of the rebels, heard not only by the Prince but also by his family, gives the film a political perspective it seemed to have lost. But it is a summary gesture, a homage to the revolutionary causes in which Visconti believes but is not involved.

NOTES

1. See previous chapter, note 5.
2. *Luchino Visconti: Il Gattopardo*, in *Dal Soggetto al Film*, Cappelli.
3. In *Ossessione*, *Senso*, *Rocco and his Brothers*, and *Vaghe Stelle dell'Orsa* respectively.
4. One of the most fascinating things about the whole sequence is the way in which the fourteen rooms of the palace are used as a single set. The use of pillars, walls, and doorways to block out or open up the scenes means that a single camera movement can have the syntactic effect of a series of cuts.
5. The super-human figure of the Prince has one parallel in Visconti's work, and that is the representation of Blasetti in *Bellissima*. Detached figures, whether above, beneath, or on the margins of the action, exist in most of his films, but most often they appear, like Blasetti, only in one scene. One whose presence is felt throughout a large part of the action is Pietro, the young doctor in *Vaghe Stelle dell'Orsa*. Pietro, by class and by temperament an outsider, is an outsider to the main action, but he observes and, unlike the naïve Andrew, understands from a distance. If *Lo Straniero* is at all faithful to the novel—or even to what one imagines Visconti's interpretation of it will be—we shall have yet another variation there of the observer motif. None of these, however, offers a complete parallel. *The Leopard* remains the only film in which one character remains permanently above the action and critical of it, and at the same time appears to receive endorsement from the author.

7: White Nights

When *White Nights* first came out it encountered a hostile reception almost everywhere. Particularly in Italy it was seen, and still occasionally is, as evidence that Visconti had now finally abandoned neo-realism and indeed realism of any kind. *Ergo* he was no longer a serious director. At ten years distance these accusations have lost most of their force. Two years after *White Nights*, Visconti reaffirmed his seriousness by making *Rocco and his Brothers*. His subsequent development and a reassessment of his early work have shown that his relationship with realism has always been ambiguous. At the same time realism has ceased to seem the unqualified aesthetic good that it was felt to be in the 1940s and 1950s. *White Nights* has come to be seen, in these terms, no longer as a betrayal but as an exquisite interlude in Visconti's career, charming but insignificant.

This new state of critical affairs is, if anything, worse than the first. The argument that *White Nights* was a betrayal of neo-realism was at least grounded in a solid aesthetic theory, and corresponded to fact. *White Nights*, with its deliberate irrealism, comes at the end of a steady development, through *Bellissima* and *Senso*, away from the naturalistic and realistic approaches of *Ossessione* and *La Terra Trema*. The new empiricism, on the other hand, is based on no theory at all, but on one or two unsystematic factual observations used to reinforce subjective feelings of like and dislike.

With a director as important and as complex as Visconti it is extremely unsafe to make pronouncements, based on external criteria, about what is major and what is minor in his work. One's criteria can only be the structures revealed in each film and the way these can be related to each other in the total context of the author's work. In this perspective there can be no major and minor, distinguished by subject, "truth to reality", "profundity of insight", or any such atomistically determined characteristic. The most one can say is that, after close analysis, a particular film seems to add little to one's understanding, but even that can be deceptive. Repetition is itself significant, and the recurrence of motifs often reveals more about a director's work than the introduction of ideas which are new and potentially distracting. This is obviously not the only way in which films can be judged. It has self-imposed limitations and would not do, for example, for a study of films in which there is no connecting thread of distinct authorship. But where one is concerned with an author whose work does show some form of internal coherence however slight, it is at the very least a necessary preliminary to judgment.

To rescue *White Nights* from the limbo of partial damnation into which it has been cast, an argument must be put forward which relates it to two basic co-ordinates, chronological and structural. This entails, in the first place, emphasising the continuity of Visconti's work and the place of *White Nights* in the continuous process of his artistic development. But it is also necessary to break down the film into its constituent elements and show both how these elements are formed, within the film, into an autonomous and equilibrated whole, and, furthermore, how they relate to and occasionally oppose the corresponding elements in Visconti's other films.

The story of *White Nights* is basically the same as that of the Dostoievsky story from which it is adapted. A lonely man (Dostoievsky, with what seems undue literary hyperbole, presents him as having no friends or acquaintances at all) meets a lonely girl. He is lonely for social reasons; he is a stranger and a newcomer. She is lonely because she has always lived in isolation, even in the heart of the city, and her loneliness is intensified voluntarily because she is in love with a man whom she does not expect ever to return to her but who continues to occupy her life to the exclusion of any other possible relationship. Incredibly, at the end of the film, the lover does return. She is vindicated, and the man who had befriended her and had hoped for her love is left behind, more isolated than before.

In the general history of film *White Nights* is mainly interesting for helping to launch the inimitable Marcello Mastroianni on his successful career as an unsuccessful lover, and for its influence on the New French Cinema, particularly Resnais, after 1958. Within Visconti's *œuvre*, however, it occupies an absolutely central position. It looks forward to *The Leopard* in its rendering of subjectivity by visual style, and to *Vaghe Stelle dell'Orsa* in its use of a complex metaphorical structure. But it also stands at the end of a line, and after making *White Nights* Visconti enters on a period of involution, doubling back on himself and recapitulating themes and motifs first developed earlier in his career.

The almost linear process which finishes with *White Nights* can best be characterised by focusing on a single aspect: Visconti's movement away from natural surroundings to artificial. The setting is always a prime determinant, and the characters have the kind of reality that is established for them by their surroundings, by the physical background and the social scene. Only in *Ossessione* are the surroundings entirely natural, real places presented with a minimum of expressive distortion, people fulfilling natural and unforced social roles. In this sense Visconti's abandonment of realism begins with his use of semi-expressionist techniques in *La Terra Trema*. In the creation and manipulation of a bizarre social world in *Bellissima* and still more in the operatic and idealising style of *Senso*, Visconti is steadily moving towards the position of *White Nights*.

This position is extreme. Natural locations are entirely eliminated, and the whole film was shot on a carefully constructed studio set, whose only concession to realism was that it is modelled on Livorno and not St. Petersburg. Whereas in *Senso* the settings

White Nights: the meeting on the bridge

were real but managed accidentally to look artificial, because of the lighting and the disjunction of character and background, here the setting both *is* artificial and is clearly intended to be seen as such. This is partly due to the photography and lighting, which produce an unexpectedly grainy look, dreamy in its effect, with unusually soft definition and carefully graduated contrasts reminiscent of the *réalisme poétique* of Carné. But it is also due to the presentation of the characters in relation to their surroundings.

We have already noticed how in Visconti's films, right from the start, people other than the direct protagonists tend to be grouped together as a sort of chorus, occupying a middle ground between the foreground personalities and the physical background. In *White Nights* the division is somewhat different. There is no clearly articulated social structure to which either the main or the episodic figures can be related. The episodic figures are part of the background, props of the physical setting, which occasionally burst into life in moments of tension between the main characters. The absence of a proper middle ground puts the protagonists into direct relation with the background, and although they are also defined socially, if only in a rudimentary and summary fashion, the primary definition is offered by the physical setting. *White Nights* is a classic illustration of André Bazin's dictum that, in the cinema, "toute la réalité est sur le même plan".[1] The characters move through the background and within the space set out for them by the camera's visual field, and are established for what they are by the general sense of irreality which pervades the initial pictorial presentation.

Bazin's statement, however, was intended also as a norm, which enabled him to criticise not only montage effects *à la* Eisenstein but also the cinematic presentation of Molière with Comédie-Française actors performing and reciting an artificial text in an inappropriate naturalistic setting. In a case like that, he went on to argue, theatre should be performed as theatre. But it is precisely one of the major differences between theatre and cinema that in the former all of reality is *not* on the same level, and the characters are not and cannot be perfectly congruent with their setting. The presentation of *White Nights* is also theatrical. The characters emerge from the background and play out their roles against it. They are figures on a stage as well as figures in a landscape.

In Dostoievsky's story the sense of irreality was produced by literary means, a first-person interior monologue whose fixed point is the state of mind of the speaker as he writes down his memories and which moves off into a realm of distant reverie. Visconti rejects the literary device of interior monologue, though he had used it in *Senso*, and relies for his effect on the cinematic and theatrical effects studied above. The result, as a French critic has noted,[2] is "plus de rêve et moins de rêverie". It is also rather more complex, since it lacks the temporal and psychological fixed point of the moment of memory. Except for a couple of brief scenes in flashback which respect Dostoievsky's strict subordination of the girl's own memories to the basic narrative, there is a free continuum between an "objective" camera's-eye view and the contrasting subjective visions of the two characters. What there is, however, to distinguish the viewpoints and to act as a point of reference for the narrative, equivalent to Dostoievsky's literary fixed point, is a specifically cinematic device: a complex spatial metaphor, which gives a key to the construction of the film.

This central spatial metaphor is provided by a canal which divides the set into two distinct worlds and the bridge over the canal which links the two halves together. The division is suggestive rather than categorical, metaphor rather than allegory. On one side of the bridge is the world in which Natalia lives with her blind grandmother: on the other side is the vital life of the city. This spatial division does more than isolate the girl geographically. It is the symbol for a whole series of contrasts—between memory and actuality, public and private, illusion and reality. The girl's world is peopled only by herself, her grandmother, the old lady's companion and helper, and the mysterious lodger whom the girl loves. It is a world of personal and private relationships existing partly in reality, partly in the memory, and partly in imagination. By being drawn across the bridge and towards the girl, the man is forced to partake of the fairy-tale atmosphere of this private world, to share

its illusions and mix them with his own. But he never fully enters into it, and it preserves a fantasy quality even for him. He knows of it through her, that is through her imagination, and his picture of it is compounded of imaginative elements, partly from her fantasy, partly from his own.

If he is to succeed in winning her for himself and away from the memory of her lost lover, he has to draw her back across the bridge, into the flesh and blood actuality of the world outside. Behind the dynamic subjective contrast of the illusion of two wills —the girl's that her lover will come back: the man's that he can draw her away from herself and her private isolation—stand the static and objective contrasts, many of which echo antinomies basic to Visconti's other films. Thus, while the girl's private world is also one of timeless past and future, historically continuous, the world on the other side of the bridge is specifically modern and actual. It is a world of bright lights, juke boxes, and neon signs, full of mundane self-assertion, in sharp contrast to the house that the girl inhabits, filled with worn-out Oriental carpets being laboriously restored.

Various of the antinomies which Visconti establishes in his other films—between guilty passion and easy love, permanence and transience, past and present, traditional and pop culture—find specific expression in the two worlds of *White Nights*. A simple example will suffice to demonstrate the part that these static contrasts play in the construction of the film. The lodger invites the girl and her grandmother to the opera to hear Rossini's *Barber of Seville*, much to the old lady's delight since she remembers the opera from her childhood and even manages, in a cracked voice, to sing snatches from one of the arias. They all go along together, a cosy family group immersing itself in an artistic experience which represents a permanent cultural continuity. When Mastroianni takes her out, on the other hand, it is the cinema he first thinks of. They do not in fact go, because it is too late. But the following evening, when they have time to spare, they go to a café, and finish up dancing, in a clumsy but frenetic fashion, to a record of Bill Haley and his Comets. In impersonal surroundings, separated from each other by

125

the movements of the other dancers, they manage with difficulty to establish some kind of personal contact. The scene is vivid enough, and brilliantly staged: but it is curiously unreal. It has actuality, but of a transient kind. It is dated by the music, quite emphatically: 1957. By contrasting it with the opera sequence Visconti is not just telling us something about his taste in music. He is both illuminating the dynamic contrasts between the protagonists and providing a framework of understanding. The opera/pop contrast is neither isolated nor incidental, it is an essential part of a symbolic structure in forming the film.

What the structure is becomes clearer if one looks at the working out of the plot. Natalia's world is effectively timeless. Her lover has promised to return within the year, thus intruding an element of temporality into the affair, after which the continuity will be restored. The year is up, and she goes every evening patiently to wait for him on one of the bridges over the canal, at the point of junction with the outside world. It is here that the young man, Mario, finds her, weeping because another evening has gone by and her lover has not returned. On the grounds that she has been pestered by some youths on a motor-cycle, he insists on taking her home. Reluctantly, because it looks like a pick-up, she allows him to accompany her, but not beyond the door. She arranges to meet him again the following evening, but at the last minute changes her mind. She tries to avoid him, and when he corners her gives him a line about not wanting to appear frivolous by accepting appointments with strangers. They sit on the canal bank and she tells him about her life, the narrative merging into images of the scene she is describing. He objects to the story, which he finds implausible, and particularly to her assumption that it is all perfectly ordinary. All the time she is trying to force her version on to him. She talks compulsively about herself and alternates between excitement and despair, and between holding off and encouraging the unfortunate Mario. He protests ineffectually. His perception of her is clouded by his illusion that he can prise her away from the world of her imagination. He is enough of a dreamer to submit to this illusion and to allow himself to be attracted to her and to her world. But at the same time he belongs on the other side. To her he can never mean anything. She is as blind to the ordinary world as he is to the power of her fantasy. When he persuades her that, if she knows where her lover is, she should write to him, telling him that she is waiting, she appears to let herself be guided by him; then, when they have completed a draft together, she produces a fair copy, already written, of the same letter, which she asks him to post. She has, in fact, imposed her vision completely. He responds irrationally to the situation. When she has left, he destroys the letter as if by doing so he could shatter her vision and replace it with his own. Just before he does this a prostitute saunters by and smiles at him. His determination reinforced, he tears up the letter and drops the pieces into the canal.

The third evening, in contrast to the last, is dominated by Mario, his initiative and images of his world. The figure of the prostitute occurs again, and this time Mario nearly succumbs to the alternative she offers. She is almost a permanent feature of the landscape, moving to and fro between the bridge and a near-by café, and tantalising Mario with the promise of something more tangible, if more temporary, than his fairy-tale romance. Nor is she the only erotic distraction that offers itself. As Mario stands looking in the window of a café an attractive blonde inscribes a large "Ciao" in the condensation on the glass. He seems to be considering picking her up when Natalia appears, accusing him in a neurotic way of trying to avoid her, which he in fact is. Once again he allows himself to be encouraged. He takes her to the café and starts telling her about himself. She isn't listening: so he asks her to dance. The scene that follows is a set piece of amazing virtuosity. Not only does it contain one of the best stagings of a rock number ever produced in the cinema: it also manages to convey the different relationships of the characters to each other and to the world. Mario, despite his stuffy remarks about growing old, is relaxed and happy and even succeeds in monopolising the floor for a Jerry Lewis type send-up of the star dance. Natalia, meanwhile, grows more and more hysterical. The music stops, and she begins to calm down. Then, suddenly, hearing that it is past ten o'clock, the hour of her nightly appointment, she rushes out to look for her lover on the bridge.

In reaction to this act of desertion, Mario lets himself be picked up by the prostitute, but draws back at the last minute. He is still a victim of his dream. When the woman starts screaming at him for taking advantage of her, figures emerge from all round and start beating him up—despite her immediate reversal of attitude and pleas that they leave him alone. She has a code and a sense of honour which Natalia lacks, but in other respects there is a marked similarity between the figurations. Both are prone to sudden reversals of feeling and to outbursts of near-hysteria: both represent a snare in which the man allows himself to be caught. But the prostitute is more straightforward in her demands, freer with what she has to give, and ultimately more generous.

Formally, the scene with the prostitute repeats the pattern of the scene with the girl behind the plate-glass window a few minutes earlier, and the rest of the pattern then repeats itself as well. Natalia reappears, not having found her lover. Once again Mario falls under her spell; once again he manages to persuade himself that he is making progress; and once again he is cruelly deluded, this time definitively.

On her return Natalia gives the impression of being a pure mythomaniac. She is now overcome by despair, and has refashioned her image of her lover completely. She sees herself as having been deceived, and is perversely pleased when Mario confesses to having destroyed the letter. She interprets the world according to her preconceived notions of what she wants it to be, and is capable of swinging violently from one extreme to another. In her new mood she is utterly compliant to Mario's proposals. He takes her out in a boat, to a place along the canal where lovers go to be alone. But the place is occupied—not by lovers, but by homeless families sheltering from the cold. It begins to snow. She is ecstatic: all the time she regards the weather as something that exists to do her bidding, and now she expects the people on the bank to share her delight in the spectacle of the falling snowflakes. They get out of the boat and go for a walk, with Mario reflecting on how the snow

White Nights: the meeting in the snow, and the carpet workshop

seems to fall like a bridal veil on his new beloved. His illusion is now as complete as he took hers to be. They start walking back. Below them on a bridge over the canal stands a muffled figure in a hat and heavy coat. He calls out, quietly and imperiously, "Natalia!" Her trust has been finally vindicated, and against a setting where the snow has obliterated the details of the landscape and contingency and actuality have been abolished, where everything is fairy-tale, she runs down the hill to meet him, leaving Mario alone, befriending the same stray dog that he had encountered and befriended at the very beginning of the film.

Throughout the film we are faced by the opposition of two levels of reality, the actual and the ideal. The actual is characterised by transience, modernity, social dissociation: by pop music, the youths on motor-bikes, the prostitute and her clients, the passers-by. The ideal, by its nature, is less readily concretised in particular images. It is the product of the transforming power of the imagination. The same contrast as is expressed in the spatial division of the film exists within the characters themselves. On the level of actuality Natalia is a hysterical little bitch. In her imagination she is the ideal faithful beloved and her lover will return to her because she believes in her love. The extraordinary thing about the film is that she is allowed to triumph, that the ideal becomes reality. *White Nights* is not a sentimental film. On the level of observation it is lucid and even realistic. Little details like the grandmother's taste for particularly gruesome murder stories, as well as the unsparing characterisation of the heroine, give even the old world on the far side of the bridge a firm base in realistic observation. But the film is marked throughout by a voluntary idealisation of the subject. Stylistically this comes out in the exaggeration of visual and psychological details, and in the extreme formality of the spatial and temporal composition. In thematic terms it is expressed in the constant tension and dialectical contrasts between the characters and their conflicting visions of the world and themselves.

If this is so, then Visconti's anti-realism goes deeper than is generally realised. *White Nights* is perhaps an extreme example of this tendency. Its spiritual descendants are to be found in the works of Jacques Demy, *Lola* and *Les Parapluies de Cherbourg*, and in Resnais's *L'Année Dernière à Marienbad*. But within Visconti's work before *White Nights* aspects of the same tendency can be seen operating in *Senso*, notably in the way the world of art (opera and painting) is used as an ideal image and a corrective against which actuality is to be judged. Still other aspects remain latent throughout his later work, to find their most explicit expression in *Vaghe Stelle dell'Orsa*, which Visconti made some eight years later, in 1965.

NOTES

1. *Qu'est-ce que le Cinéma?* Vol. I *Ontologie et Langage*, Paris 1958, p. 160 n.
2. Philippe Demonsablon in *Cahiers du Cinéma*, June 1958 vol. 14, no. 84, p. 47.

8: Vaghe Stelle dell'Orsa

The importance of *White Nights* in Visconti's development, so often misconstrued by his critics, really becomes clear with the appearance of *Vaghe Stelle dell'Orsa*, the latest of his films to be released in this country. In the intervening period he made *Rocco and his Brothers*, which we shall examine later, *Il Lavoro*, and *The Leopard*. In discussing *White Nights*, I described this period as one of involution, in which Visconti returns to subjects and stylistic motifs first treated in his earlier films and now redeveloped in a new and often more complex fashion. With *Rocco and his Brothers*, most conspicuously, Visconti seems to be making almost an abrupt about-turn, away from theatrical artifice, memory, and the past, and back to a contemporary and realistic study of the social problems which first engaged his attention in *La Terra Trema*. In this perspective *White Nights* looked very much like a dead end, an aesthetic diversion from which Visconti was at pains to extricate himself and which left little or no mark on the subsequent progress of his career. If *Vaghe Stelle dell'Orsa* has helped us to revise our estimate of *White Nights* and to rescue it from critical cold storage, it is also true, however, as a necessary corollary that the later film cannot be situated without reference to the earlier.

Like *White Nights*, *Vaghe Stelle dell'Orsa* has a complicated structure which is not simply that of the plot. In *White Nights* the plot is very simple. What action there is depends for its significance entirely on things outside it. The film is based on the contrast of

two subjective visions, one of which is finally vindicated. But the last-minute vindication of the girl's faith does not annul the rest. The enigma remains, and with it the structural contrasts thrown up by the plot and made concrete in a central metaphor, that of the bridge connecting two worlds.

In *Vaghe Stelle dell'Orsa* the plot is more intricate, but as in *White Nights* it is motivated from the outside—by two events which may or may not have happened in the past: incest by an adolescent couple of sister and brother, and the betrayal of their Jewish father to the Nazis by their mother and her lover. Unlike *White Nights*, however, the enigma is never resolved. Again, the action in *Vaghe Stelle dell'Orsa* is bounded by an extended metaphor, in this case linking past, present, and future.

The film starts with a brief pre-credit scene in Geneva, where Sandra and her American husband are giving a party. The smart international guests mill around, talking in English and French. A pianist starts playing César Franck's Prelude, a tense piece of music whose romantic turbulence is kept in check by an iron vest of classical form. For Sandra, however, the symbolism of the music is more specific. She looks distraught, but says nothing to her husband about the cause, which we learn later is the association of the music with her mother, a former concert pianist now in a mental home.

The next day Sandra and Andrew leave for Italy. The car speeds away from Geneva, across the barrier of the Alps, swallowing up distance, with an unexpected zoom shot on to a flock of white birds round a meadow; thence along the motorways of Northern Italy. Outside Florence it slows down and plunges into a narrow country lane, flanked by hedges, dark and shadowy. Eventually they reach Volterra, a decaying town on the edge of a crumbling volcanic precipice. Only the omnipresent Coca-Cola advertisements reflect the presence of the twentieth century.

The journey from Geneva is a journey backwards in time, away from modernity into history. It is also, for Sandra, a journey into her own past. She and Andrew are going to attend a ceremony in which the garden of her home is to be turned into a public park,

135

dedicated to the memory of her father, who died in Auschwitz. The dedication is to be both an act of homage and an exorcism, a laying of family ghosts.

But the ghosts refuse to be laid. There seems to be a kind of curse on the family at Volterra. Other members of the family refuse to attend the ceremony. One who does turn up is Gianni, Sandra's brother. Andrew attempts to discover the cause of family rifts and tensions and to settle them in a sensible way. But he only succeeds in exacerbating the conflicts and in forcing on himself a horrifying discovery—that of supposed incest between Sandra and Gianni. Andrew leaves for New York, hoping that Sandra will follow him. Gianni threatens suicide in a desperate attempt to win Sandra and dies. At the end of the film Sandra, her own ghosts exorcised, stands at the ceremony next to her heavily sedated mother, preparing to complete her journey into a safe future with Andrew.

The initial spatio-temporal metaphor is a key without which the film is incomprehensible. For *Vaghe Stelle dell'Orsa* is not an easy film, partly because its construction is so complex and so enigmatic and partly because its melodramatic surface discourages attempts at deeper analysis. As is usual with Visconti, the melodramatics are not incidental but essential. There are, however, a number of red herrings drawn across the path by, among others, the author himself which need to be disposed of before the film can be properly understood.

A major stumbling-block to appreciation is the result of what can only be seen as a gross error of casting—Claudia Cardinale's performance as the heroine. What Visconti wanted apparently was someone whose enigmatic beauty could express Sandra's crisis of identity and the destructive power of someone who in a personal sense is non-existent.[1] It is not an easy part to play and Cardinale nowhere near gets the measure of it. Bad acting or non-acting can often be turned to advantage in the cinema, where the actor's function is not necessarily that of an interpreter. The enigmatic character of Sandra required a face that respected the enigma and did not attempt to solve it by irrelevant subtleties of expression. But Cardinale is not really enigmatic. Her attempts to "fill in" a part which precisely demanded to be left empty produce a character for Sandra which is fundamentally at odds with the rest of the film. In the place of an enigma we have an ambiguity.

A second barrier to understanding lies in the literary references and echoes with which the film is beset. The title "Vaghe Stelle dell'Orsa" comes from a poem of Leopardi, *Le Ricordanze*, which is extensively quoted in the film by the brother, Gianni. It is also the title which Gianni is proposing to give to the semi-autobiographical novel he has just completed. The reference to Leopardi, the young romantic poet, isolated, despairing, dominated first by the reality then by the memory of his oppressive provincial family, is important, and would be recognised as such by an Italian audience, though more for what Visconti is telling us about Gianni than for what it says about Visconti's own cultural interests. On an English audience the point is entirely lost—particularly since the English title of *Vaghe Stelle dell'Orsa* is "Of a Thousand Delights" which bears no relation whatever to the original.

The English title does, however, introduce literary overtones of its own. Whether by accident or design, it echoes phrases from a Jacobean drama, Ford's *'Tis Pity She's a Whore*, which Visconti produced in Paris in 1961. The play has a certain similarity with the film. Incest between brother and sister is a main theme in *'Tis Pity She's a Whore*, and is also a theme of *Vaghe Stelle dell'Orsa*. A scene in the film where Gianni removes Sandra's ring echoes an incident in Ford's play.[2] But unlike the Leopardi reference, the Ford references are not intended to say anything to the spectator. They point to a continuity between Visconti's original work in the cinema and his interpretative work in the theatre, but are much less significant for the film than, say, the references to Verdi in *Senso*. If treated as important they can only mislead, by suggesting for example that *Vaghe Stelle dell'Orsa* is a film about incest—an idea which might appeal in the X-film trade but is not Visconti's.[3]

The role of incest in *Vaghe Stelle dell'Orsa* has also sparked off another risky comparison, this time with the Orestes myth, a comparison which so entranced one critic[4] that he substituted the names of the Greek heroes for those of the characters throughout

his review. The problem here is different again. The parallel, once pointed out, is obvious, but it cannot be stressed too strongly that *Vaghe Stelle dell'Orsa* is not a modern version of the *Oresteia* after the manner of Dassin's updated *Phaedra*. The connection is allusive—between the situation of the film and the myth: not between Visconti's and Aeschylus' literary telling of the story. There is no imitation of detail, no bloody axe, no footprints in the sand. There may not even have been a murder. What Visconti has done is to abstract certain elements of the saga, not necessarily the most important in the original structure, and to place them in a new structure which is entirely his own. Though the myth is important, because it provides a pattern of classic symmetry within the film, it should not be allowed to obscure the extent to which the actual working out of the pattern takes place in terms which are strictly Viscontian, and certainly not Aeschylus.

The central feature of the myth which is contained in *Vaghe Stelle dell'Orsa* is the idea of the transmission of the family curse from one generation to the next. The curse is not real in the sense of being objectified in the form of a decree of the gods. But it is felt. The mother sees her children by her first husband as being tainted by their Jewishness. The children, particularly Sandra, see their actions as a response to the betrayal of their father by their mother and stepfather. Within the film this provides a symmetrical pattern and a starting-point for the action. The assumption by the children of their parents' crime forces them together in a way which is itself interpreted by the stepfather as criminal, and the pattern of structural interaction is present whether or not crimes as such actually took place.

The situation, which the action of the film disrupts, is one of uneasy equilibrium. The family is split up. Sandra has gone to Geneva, initially to pursue an inquiry into her father's death. Subsequently she has married and, by her marriage, has withdrawn her connections with past guilt. The mother has gone mad. Gilardini, the stepfather, is content to let sleeping dogs lie and allows Gianni occasionally to plunder the family property of which Gilardini is trustee. What starts the action going in the first

Vaghe Stelle dell'Orsa: Sandra about to give Gianni her ring

instance is Sandra's obsession with her father's memory and a structural asymmetry between her and Gianni's position and that of the others.

The two couples, Gianni and Sandra and Gilardini and the mother, are in an analogous position. Gilardini and the mother are presumed guilty of an abnormal and indecent complicity in conniving at or even engineering the father's denunciation. Sandra and Gianni are suspected of complicity in their hostility to their parents and their possible incest. This complicity involves a number of real or imagined acts of betrayal, sexual, familial, and even racial. The mother has betrayed the father by taking Gilardini as a lover: Sandra betrays Andrew by her attachment to Gianni, which she has never admitted. By denouncing the father and disowning the children the mother has also betrayed the family, and her action is reciprocated by Sandra, who denounces her for what she has done. Sandra also wishes to deny the existence of any love between her and Gianni and sees her relationship as racial solidarity, brought about by the racial denunciation of the father. This in turn gives rise to counter-accusation between Gianni and Sandra. He feels she has betrayed him and their childhood: she feels he has betrayed their race.

This pattern of accusation and counter-accusation contains one asymmetrical factor, which is temporal. The mother's crime is past, and can neither be repaired nor renewed. Even her disowning of the children is no longer important, now that they have grown up. Any personal responsibility she might have is annulled by her withdrawal, possibly as a consequence of guilt, into madness. Sandra's withdrawal, again conditioned by the past, is less complete. Her hatred of her mother is still alive and potentially destructive, and her withdrawal to Geneva has left her own problems unresolved. Gianni's appearance at Volterra is sufficient both to trouble her relationship with Andrew and to reactivate the past, either directly or in the suspicious mind of Gilardini.

A further danger to the equilibrium lies in the mutual distrust that grows up between Gianni and Andrew, the brother and husband. Andrew is puzzled by the situation: the vast, echoing house, the locked doors guarding the mother's former apartment, the depth of affection between brother and sister, and the evidence of hostility in the refusal of other members of the family to attend the ceremony. Gianni is straightforwardly jealous of the man who has separated him from his sister; he is also anxious that Andrew should not discover too much, at least not immediately. He shows Andrew round Volterra, and parries his questions with devious replies. Andrew wants to know about Sandra's past, in order to understand her as she is now. Gianni contests the relevance of the past, and argues that what a person was has no bearing on what that person is and is loved for in the present. All the time he is playing a game with Andrew, tantalising him with cryptic remarks and finally distracting his attention to Pietro, the son of the estate factor and now a doctor treating the mother. Later, when they meet Pietro in a café, Andrew turns his back on him. He is now extremely confused. His suspicions have been distracted but not allayed, and he turns his hostility on to the unfortunate Pietro, without evidence and without conviction, aware that something is amiss and that Pietro is somehow connected with it.

Yet more suspicions are aroused in Andrew's mind during a scene in the Town Hall where the documents have been signed handing over the garden to the municipality. Sandra has arrived late, flustered and distraught, having just returned from seeing her mother. Gilardini obviously resents her intervention in what he feels is his business. He is convinced that Sandra's only intention is to cause trouble, and he stalks away after the signing calling out that if Sandra wants to stir it up for him, the truth will come out and will not be to her advantage. Later Andrew hears the story about Pietro again, this time from Sandra. Little things, like his insistence on being able to take movie shots of Sandra in the house when they arrive, have established both his insensitivity and his role as an intruder. His curiosity, still fairly innocent, remains obstinate and unflagging. Reluctantly Sandra shows him round the house the next day, pointing out the places where, she claims, Pietro used to leave messages for her. Niched in a statue of Cupid and Psyche in her mother's apartment is a note from Gianni, which Sandra

claims, absurdly, to be an old note from Pietro. Andrew appears to accept this, but it is no longer possible for him to be put off. As in a Hitchcock film, from being an innocent outsider he now becomes the pivot of the action. He is determined to know the facts, at whatever cost, but still preserves his naïve belief, now verging on the disingenuous, that he is acting in the common interest and that uncovering the truth will serve to heal the rifts and bring the family together.

To this end, when Sandra goes to her assignation with Gianni, Andrew sets out to find Gilardini. What Gilardini tells him we are not told. Whatever it was, Andrew's appreciation of the situation is not much altered. He determines to invite both Gilardini and Pietro to dinner, to bring about a general reconciliation. Gianni is tactful and urbane, and so at the outset is Gilardini. But a vicious remark from Sandra stings Gilardini to retaliate. He openly accuses the brother and sister of past incest. Andrew asks Gianni to deny it, which Gianni, in honesty to his present feelings and interpretation of the past, refuses to do. Andrew's response is horror, which explodes in violence. He sets about beating up Gianni to force a denial, still refusing ostensibly to believe that Gilardini's accusation is true, but at the same time convinced that there is no other explanation for what he has heard and seen. When Sandra also fails to deny it, he leaves for New York, leaving a note for Sandra that all is forgotten and asking her to join him. His search for the truth has brought him up against something which, true or not, is unacceptable, and rather than face it he is prepared to renounce his inquiry and declare that, after all, the past is not important. His reversal of his former position is surprising, particularly since he had taken part, with Sandra, in an inquiry into the Auschwitz massacres. His concern to discover the truth about her family began there. But he has no proper understanding of the meaning of the past, and his public and private attitudes contradict each other. When the past threatens him directly, he turns and runs.

The ambiguity of Andrew's situation is that he enters the film as an outsider, with no past guilt behind him. He has done nothing and has nothing to conceal. But it is his clumsy probings which

143

precipitate the confrontation between Gianni and Gilardini, and he more than anyone is responsible for the final tragedy. As a character he is both unimaginative and self-deceiving. In some ways, despite Michael Craig's very British playing of the role, he is a caricature of the Ugly American, rationalistic and uncomprehending, and liable to resort to bludgeoning violence when his superficial rationality fails him. He sees himself in a role similar to that of a management consultant sorting out the problems of a disintegrating family business. Morally his error lies in not appreciating the extent of his own involvement. He is part of the family structure and has motivations of his own as well. His psychology and his understanding of his own situation are, however, relatively insignificant, compared with his objective role. Utterly taken by surprise by events which are beyond his comprehension, he nevertheless fulfils the function allotted to him. He liberates Sandra from dependence on her family, but only at the cost of destroying the family itself.

In contrast to Andrew, Pietro plays an entirely passive role. He is used by Gianni and Sandra as a diversion, both in the past and during the film. He is perfectly aware of being used. Infatuated with Sandra as a boy, he was forced to see himself as an outsider both by his social class and by the exclusive relationship of the brother and sister. Now, as a doctor attached to the local sanatorium, he is in a position to observe the mother's madness and her relationship with her "viperish" children. He has no active role forced on him by his position, and is too intelligent, and probably knows too much, to wish to interfere of his own accord. He is not so much above as below the action, the hapless victim of Sandra and Gianni's complicity, Andrew's jealousy, Gilardini's mistrust, and the mother's rages. His role is in fact the exact obverse of Andrew's. Pietro withdraws where Andrew rushes in. Where Andrew has power without understanding, Pietro has understanding but no power.

A further mirror to Pietro is provided by Fosca, the old family maid. She, like Laura, Livia's maid in *Senso*, is both knowledgeable and an accomplice. But being an accomplice and having no social role independent of the family she serves, she is even more powerless than Pietro. Apart from his affection for Sandra, nothing binds Pietro to the family. He can observe its destruction, if not with indifference, with equanimity softened by pity. According to Gianni, Pietro studied to become a doctor because of his love for Sandra. By doing so he made himself her equal, but his position relative to the family is still subordinate, in that he is employed by Gilardini to look after the mother. Unlike Fosca, he stands to gain by waiting upon events. As an observer, with understanding but without power, he resembles 'Ntoni in *La Terra Trema* and the Prince in *The Leopard*. But whereas 'Ntoni is powerless because defeated and the Prince is losing power because he has been overtaken by events, Pietro in the same historical perspective is a representative, like Ciro in *Rocco and his Brothers*, of a new emergent class which will take over when the long agony of the aristocracy comes to an end.

Class questions apart, Pietro provides an implicit corrective to the distorted visions and conflicting rationalisations of the protagonists proper. Having no stake in the internal convolutions in which the family are tied up, he can view the whole affair without *parti pris*. For members of the family themselves, however, things are not so simple. The mother has withdrawn into madness, thumping out the César Franck Prelude and Fugue on the piano and nursing among her private wounds an especial hatred for her daughter. Gilardini, whose cautious manner suggests a man with something to hide, is concerned, ostensibly, to protect her from her children and the family as a whole from the world outside. Neither Gianni nor Sandra can accept his version of affairs, but for different reasons. To Sandra he is the man who replaced, and possibly denounced, her father. To Gianni he is rather the ravisher of his mother. The conflict between generations is complicated by differences of attitude, which are to have far-reaching consequences, between the children.

The Freudian basis of the different vision of events held by the brother and the sister is obvious. It is also one of the few direct points of contact with the Orestes myth. Significantly, the first

meeting of Gianni and Sandra takes place in the garden which is about to be dedicated to their father's memory. Sandra is silently embracing the veiled bust of her father. When Gianni enters, she turns away, and he embraces her. It looks more like the meeting of lovers than of siblings, however close the family bonds. Andrew, who supervenes looking for Sandra, is visibly embarrassed, and the surprise is heightened for the spectator by Gianni's dramatic appearance behind the iron grille of the gate leading to the garden. The important thing, however, is not the shock but the way the action portrays the relationships: Andrew's position as outsider, Sandra's obsessional cult of her father, and Gianni's love for Sandra.

The pattern of relationships revealed in this scene is further reflected in the different accounts that Gianni and Sandra give of their childhood and of the links that bind them together. Gianni has just found out that he is in love with his sister, whom he had tried to forget. It is her marriage which has made him realise that he is not capable of forgetting her, and at the time of the wedding (as Sandra discovers from Fosca) he returned secretly to his childhood home, while pretending to be in London. His discovery, as an adult, of his feelings towards his sister and their apparent continuity from his early adolescence makes him project his present feelings back on to the past. He has just completed a novel, based on their childhood together, which represents the relationship as explicitly incestuous, hoping thereby to objectify and so exorcise the guilt he feels about the past and the present passion which absorbs him. Publishing the novel will liberate him both from Sandra and from the family home by giving him for the first time emotional and financial independence.

Gianni shows Sandra the manuscript. She is horrified, and in her horror he sees the possibility of a different bargain altogether. If she refuses him permission to publish, he will offer to destroy it, on condition that she stays with him in Volterra admitting their complicity. But he has miscalculated her reaction. Her articulated response to the book is incredibly superficial. She is afraid of the gossip that will ensue, of the image that will be formed of her in other people's minds. But this does not mean that she will be prepared to stay with him if the book is suppressed. People would talk even then. Besides, these are not her real reasons. What Gianni took to be the shock of recognition and a fear of the secret truth being revealed outside, was nothing of the kind. Sandra does not recognise Gianni's version as the truth. To Sandra, rationalising the events she lived through together with Gianni many years before, all the complicity, the exclusive isolation, the secret games, even the embraces, were tokens, not of reciprocated passion but of racial solidarity. Sandra's real love is for her father, not her brother; and she hates her mother as much as she hates Gilardini. To her it is the fact of Jewishness, inherited from the father, that binds her and Gianni together, in defence of the father's memory and as a permanent gesture of defiance against the couple who betrayed him.

Sandra's version of events is as shocking to Gianni as his was to her. He does not deny his Jewish heritage, and he wears the Star of David just as she does. But to him this is not the important factor. What horrifies Gianni is Sandra's indifference, and worse, to their mother, whom he still loves. In the scene in the Town Hall he showed himself worried at the possible consequences of Sandra's precipitate visit to the mother. This visit, shown in flashback from the point of view of Sandra, gives the impression of stubborn incomprehension and implacable hatred on both sides. Later, in discussion with Sandra, Gianni openly accuses her of driving the mother mad. But he still has not got the measure of her potential for destruction. He does not realise, for example, that it could be turned against him as well.

Sandra's problem is essentially one of lack of identity. Unable to find within herself an explanation of who she is and why, she uses other people as a mirror in which to look at herself. But the image she finds reflected there offers no assurance. Only Andrew, the outsider with no knowledge of her past, allows her to feel at home in herself. Her racial self-assertion is one aspect of her crisis: another, more serious, is her determination to stamp out, during her visit to Volterra, all versions of who she is which differ from

148

her own. She demands to be vindicated, even at the cost of destroying whoever opposes her design.

Gianni no longer has this problem. He has managed, or thinks he has, through his novel, to objectify the past and at the same time to take responsibility for it. His story satisfies him, whether or not it is objectively correct. Sandra, however, is unable to lay her hands on the past and to say unequivocally—"That is what I was and this is what I am." Her Jewishness is a kind of totem which gives only a formal and petrified explanation of her to the world and to herself. Once again, as so often in Visconti's films, we are faced with the problem of a past which is inescapable and denies any possibility of advance. Only here, unlike elsewhere, it is the character's inability to understand and assume responsibility, rather than the past history itself, which creates the barrier.

As with Natalia in *White Nights*, the existential problem facing Sandra has psychological or even psycho-pathological manifestations. After the confrontation at dinner Gianni burns his manuscript, partly as a gesture confessing failure—the past is not entirely exorcised—partly as a final attempt to persuade Sandra to stay. When she comes to see him, in order to explain that she cannot stay with him, he accuses her of perverse mortification of the flesh—a charge which, though slanted and personally motivated, is accurate. The next scene shows her performing the cleansing ritual of taking a bath and shrouding herself in the purity of white in preparation for the ceremony. She winds a white veil round her head, and draws it tight over her face like a Carmelite nun as she stares into the mirror. Her choice of white appears both as an unconscious response to Gianni's charge, and as an assertion of purity and a denial of responsibility. In more objective terms, cutting out the psychological factor and relating the scene more directly to the structure, the choice of colour is even more significant. It vindicates Gianni's perception of her, and it announces the resolution of her problems.

There is a terrible irony in her denial of responsibility at this point. The ceremony takes place in the morning. After leaving Gianni's room in the evening she has sat up for a while as if undecided, with a letter from Andrew in front of her and the knowledge in the back of her mind that Gianni has threatened to kill himself, before she makes the choice it was always determined that she should make. Gianni has attempted suicide before, but mainly as a threat, relying on being discovered by Sandra or his parents before it was too late. This time Sandra elects to ignore the threat, though she must have known what it meant. As she sits writing her reply to Andrew, Gianni is writhing on the floor in his mother's bedroom struggling desperately to avert a death he never really intended to bring upon himself.

It is Pietro's intuition that leads Fosca to discover Gianni's body in the mother's apartment. As Pietro rushes down to the garden to bring the news, the ceremony has already started. The dignitaries have collected. Sandra and her mother, the survivors, are standing side by side, staring fixedly forward, while a Rabbi intones phrases in Hebrew about resurrection and the eternal life. The scene is bitterly ironic. Gianni now is dead, and the Rabbi's words, after the scene of Gianni's agony, have a hollow ring about them. And not only is Gianni dead, but the father, in the midst of this apotheosis of his memory, is undergoing a second death in Sandra's consciousness. Sandra, like her mother, has achieved a kind of dubious liberation. The family, as such, no longer exists.

The film ends here. There is no further scene to parallel the opening sequence in Geneva. As I suggested in connection with *Senso*, the drama, once it has acquired its momentum, works towards its own resolution and is self-contained. But the structure of the film is sufficiently transparent, and its outside references sufficiently explicit, to enable certain conclusions to be drawn which exceed the narrowly defined limits of the family tragedy. The family has destroyed itself from inside, but only when it had long lost its cohesiveness and its function. Since the death of the father, a scientist, and the madness of the mother, a concert pianist, it has nothing to give to the world. Gilardini, whose main job is to hold together the estate, is a mere administrator. His intrusion into the hereditary group forces the children unnaturally together. Gianni is a romantic, whose ideal self-image is deceived

by reality: he supplements an inadequate income as a gossip columnist by periodic raids on the property. Sandra's choice of a job in Geneva was dictated by piety to her father's memory. Her only hope now lies in breaking with the past. Andrew, the American, is the means through which she can do this. Her survival is not so much *trasformismo* as submergence. She can take nothing with her into the new world except what she has to offer to Andrew.

Pietro and Andrew are the inheritors; Andrew because he can absorb Sandra, Pietro because the destruction of the family is the end of a world in which his only place was as a subordinate. This brings us back to the metaphor at the beginning of the film. The journey into the past must be interpreted macrocosmically. It is not only the family past but an entire past world that Andrew and Sandra are visiting in Volterra. When Gianni is showing Andrew round the town, they sit on the edge of one of the *balze*, a steep eroding cliff overlooking a volcanic landscape. Erosion has begun to eat into the town. The Camaldolese friars have been forced to abandon their monastery. Volterra, like the family, is slowly crumbling away.

Erosion of a different kind threatens the town from a different direction. Isolated though it is, Volterra shows all the usual signs of the advance of modern civilisation—Coca-Cola advertisements stuck on the wall of a house by the road, a juke box in a café blaring out the pop message, albeit in a half-hearted Italian form, into the streets. When Gianni and Andrew return to the house on the first evening, the music follows them. "Io che non vivo senza te," the singer mourns, almost too pointedly—"I who cannot live without you"—as the camera cuts from Gianni to Andrew to Sandra asleep in their beds.[5] The ciné-camera which Andrew brings with him is another emblem of the new world, not so much in its role as a technical toy, but because, in Andrew's handling of it, it is a denial of history. "Truth twenty-four times a second", in Godard's phrase,[6] is unhistorical and unanalytical truth, which is one possible reason for Sandra's resentment at being photographed. It is significant therefore that the camera belongs to

Andrew, the only character who is prepared to believe that history is bunk and who represents, on a personal plane, the cultural levelling process by which Volterra is being overtaken.

Enough has been said about the symbolic structure of *Vaghe Stelle dell'Orsa* to indicate the extent to which the film transcends the banality of what seem at first sight to be its themes. It remains only to consider the parallel question of style and the relationship to the structure of the melodramatic presentation of the action.

One or two basic observations should be made first. The print of the film which has circulated in England has acquired a muddy texture in the process of duping and copying. The clarity and high contrasts apparently intended by Visconti have therefore been lost. The contrasts of black and white are very important in the film, both for sensory effect (the action takes place in high summer) and symbolically. The symbolism is not that of the traditional moral opposition between the forces of light and and forces of darkness. It can best be described as a kind of visual extremism which counterpoints the extreme situation of the characters. The light dazzles and the darkness obscures. There is no middle term, no possibility of nuance in assessing the scene.[7]

The camera work too is emphatic. The camera is unusually mobile for a Visconti film, and there are a number of zoom shots. (Visconti's normal preference is for slow tracks and the maximum of movement within the frame.) The effect, particularly of the zooms, is a kind of forced animation, very unlike the rest of his work. In *White Nights* there is a similar occasional forcing of the pace, but it is not produced by the camera. Here, in *Vaghe Stelle dell'Orsa*, camera and cutting techniques are used to attract attention. Some of the effects are amazingly crude, but they are never out of place. The obtrusive camera work is part of the mode of presentation. Like the use of heavy *chiaroscuro* in the lighting it can best be described, not in any pejorative sense, as Baroque.

The art-historical analogy with the painting of the sixteenth and seventeenth centuries helps to explain the question of the so-called "melodramatic" quality of *Vaghe Stelle dell'Orsa*. The problems facing the Mannerist and Baroque painters were complex and

Vaghe Stelle dell'Orsa: the crumbling landscape

unparalleled. But in one respect at least their experience is relevant and illuminating. The painters of Raphael's generation had perfected the art of composition and of representation of the human figure. They had divinised the human and humanised the divine. One of the problems facing their successors was that of expressing a more tortured and dramatic conception of human/divine relations without falling back on earlier representational techniques. The Madonna and the Saints could now be perfectly and naturalistically represented as super-human people. But they were not just individuals who could be idealised. Their roles in the Catholic system exceeded their simple human individuality, and the means of their presentation had to express them in their transcendent role, with all the tensions and dramatisations that this entailed.

The parallel with Visconti is obvious. We have met the problem before in relation to the conflict of ideality and reality in *Senso* and *White Nights*. Within *Vaghe Stelle dell'Orsa* we have already seen how Pietro, though insignificant as an individual, nevertheless has a historical role of great importance. We have also seen how the pathology of Gianni's incestuous feeling and Sandra's suspected masochism relates upwards and inwards to problems of a different order, not transcendent as in Catholic Baroque, but historical and existential. The Baroque and the melodrama are not intended to magnify the pathological aspects to the exclusion of the rest, but to transform them. A psychological study of incest is precisely what *Vaghe Stelle dell'Orsa* is not. Had the style of the film been naturalistic it would have been reasonable to have understood the film in that way. But with the stylistic implications what they are, the error is inexcusable.

NOTES

1. See *Luchino Visconti: Vaghe Stelle dell'Orsa* in *Dal Soggetto al Film* Cappelli, and also review by Gordon Gow in *Films and Filming*, December 1965.
2. "FLORIO: Where's the ring,
   That which your mother, in her will, bequeathed,
   And charged you on her blessing not to give it
   To any but your husband? Send back that.
   ANABELLA: I have it not.
   FLORIO: Ha! have it not; where is it?
   ANABELLA: My brother in the morning took it from me,
   Said he would wear it today."

   Act 2, Sc. vi.
3. Gordon Gow, *Films and Filming*, cited above.
4. Richard Roud in *Sight and Sound*, Winter 1965–6.
5. It is perhaps worth pointing out that the *words* of this song in Italian are a great deal more mournful and sentimental than those of the Dusty Springfield version "You don't have to say you love me". The fact that the tune is the same can easily mislead English spectators into reading in an irony which is not in fact present in the film.
6. Put into the mouth of Bruno in *Le Petit Soldat*, but representative of Godard's position then if not now.
7. A technical feature of a different kind worth drawing attention to here is the difference in acting style between the representatives of the two generations. As Gilardini and the mother, Renzo Ricci and Marie Bell, both of whom have mainly theatrical training and experience, *act* much more than Cardinale and Jean Sorel.

9: Rocco and his Brothers

There is a strange, rather unrealistic, scene in *La Terra Trema* where a man arrives in the village, wanders around talking to people, and then leaves in a boat taking with him a group of young men, destination uncertain. Among these young men is Cola Valastro. Before leaving he has a conversation with his brother 'Ntoni which, according to Visconti, was improvised on the spot, and in which the narrow geographical frontiers of the fisherman's world are clearly affirmed. Cola is embarking for the North, "al continente", symbolised by Naples, the *Ultima Thule* of the fisherman's vision. This scene, though it fits uneasily into the tight structure of *La Terra Trema,* was soon vindicated historically. In the boom years of the 1950s and early 1960s ever-increasing numbers of men and families began to emigrate from stagnant rural areas in the South towards the expanding industrial centres of Northern Italy. Despised (as savages) and distrusted (as black labour) by the Northerners, ignorant of the world of the golden cities for which they were heading, they ended up for the most part as an insecure, disillusioned, ghetto-living sub-proletariat on the fringes of the great industrial complexes. It is their problem, and that of the society to which they have to adapt, that provides the starting-point for *Rocco and his Brothers.*

Rocco and his Brothers was made in 1959, immediately after the radical aesthetic experiment of *White Nights,* and is a deliberate step backwards, the first stage of Visconti's moment of involution.

It is, in a sense, a sequel to *La Terra Trema* and a substitute for those episodes of that film which Visconti still regrets never having been able to make. But in the years that elapsed between the two films Visconti, like Italy itself, had moved on. The subject proposed for the new film was too unwieldy for it to be possible to combine a compact narrative with documentary (or anthropological) treatment. No one would have backed such a project if it had been put forward. In any case Visconti had no intention of being caught again in the trap of documentarism. From the moment of the film's inception, the complexity of its subject was reflected in a complexity of treatment unparalleled in Visconti's work. In addition to Suso Cecchi D'Amico, Visconti's regular and constant collaborator on all his films since *Bellissima*, a number of other scriptwriters were called in during the many stages of the elaboration of the narrative. Though the nucleus of the story was original, the final script incorporated moments of literary inspiration ranging from Dostoievsky and Thomas Mann through Verga to the Milanese stories of Giovanni Testori. The building up of the story was contributed to by various hands, but the ultimate control at every stage rested with Visconti himself, and the final shape of the film reflects the sum of his artistic experience up to that date—not only *La Terra Trema* but *Ossessione* and *Bellissima* and, above all, *Senso*.

The lessons inherent in Visconti's experience make themselves felt in two ways: in the construction of a human drama out of a historical situation, and in his choice of actors. Although its subject sounds like a return to *La Terra Trema* (perhaps an "Episodio della Città"), in style and in ideological content *Rocco and his Brothers* is much more a continuation of *Senso*. Visconti has described his form of cinema as "anthropomorphic".[1] Essentially what this means is that the totality of a historical situation, both its static form and the process of its evolution, is crystallised in certain human figurations and in the development of a human drama. (If this sounds just a complicated way of stating a truism, one has only to look at all the directors with whom this is not the case.) In *La Terra Trema* this anthropomorphism is suppressed by the view that Visconti is obliged to take of his subject—a geographical location—and the way this view is expressed from the ground up by the film's protagonists—the natural inhabitants of Aci-Trezza. In *La Terra Trema* the characterisation of 'Ntoni is unique. He is the only character whose responses are on the level required to extend the film on to the level of a historical consciousness and who provides an anthropomorphic figuration of the kind Visconti was aiming at. For the rest the film remains fundamentally a documentary study of a place which is taken to contain within its frontiers an example of a universal form of social exploitation, and its characters do not emerge from their particular and passive roles as elements of the social and economic system. *Rocco and his Brothers*, like *Senso*, aims to go beyond the limits imposed by a sociological viewpoint of this type. It is a condensed and dramatic highlighting of a particular moment of history. Its geographical and social boundaries (Milan in the 1950s; an immigrant family) are the result of a tremendous effort of historical concentration. The private events which it narrates mirror the tensions of a wider historical situation, but only indirectly, through the consciousness of the participants. The drama which then explodes within the family and the subsequent tragedy is brought about by the participants themselves, and is an active expression of the contradictions inherent in their condition.

Visconti's choice of actors to express his theme was at first sight disconcerting: the mother of the Pafundi family to be played by Katina Paxinou, who is Greek; Renato Salvatori, Alain Delon, Spiros Focas, and Max Cartier as four of her sons; plus Claudia Cardinale and Annie Girardot as fiancées and mistresses. This distribution reflects to a certain extent no doubt the producer's insistence on a star line-up. But many of the choices were clearly Visconti's, notably Delon in the part of Rocco, and show him continuing the pattern set in *Bellissima* and *Senso* of using actors for their persona as well as for their professional skill. Renato Salvatori, for example, besides being a very good and incidentally very subtle actor, has exactly the physique and facial characteristics to convey the charm and gradual disintegration of Simone, the second brother. On any grounds, naturalistic or other, he was an obvious choice. But Delon as Rocco was less obvious. Quite apart from the fact that, like Paxinou and Girardot, he is not Italian, which meant that the film would have to be post-synchronised,[2] Delon is far too fragile physically to be credible as either a peasant (which is what he starts as) or a professional boxer (which is what he becomes).

Visconti's judgment can, I think, be vindicated, in terms of the requirements of his anthropomorphic ideal. He chooses actors to fit into a role, not to conform to a type or merge into an environment. Whereas the neo-realist requirement was for someone ideally representative of a type of character drawn from their observation and was best filled in many cases by someone who actually was what they were supposed to represent, Visconti's demand is for a more complex figuration. In the first place his characters are not typical members of a class, but individuals. These individuals, in their relations with other characters in the film, then represent something that goes beyond their simple individuality. What is required of the actor is to incarnate the idea of the character, in both its individual and supra-individual aspects, and to project it. If a professional technique is needed to interpret a role which is not simply drawn from life, from the director's point of view the actor's physical appearance is equally important for the use he can make of it independent of any effort of psychological interpretation on the actor's part. The choice of Delon is a case in point. He is meant to look fragile, and it is essential to our understanding of Rocco that we should realise this. It is not so much Delon who is miscast in the role, as Rocco who is miscast in his environment. Both as a person and for what he represents, Rocco is ill-adapted to the world in which he lives and incapable of carrying the burden he assumes upon himself.

The argument about casting has further implications. To say that the actor incarnates the idea of a character raises the problem of the relation of the sign to the signified over the film as a whole. In a film, where the units of language cannot be isolated and given specific and unambiguous meanings or functions, there is always a

possibility that the translation into images will obscure some intended meanings and create others not originally intended. Intentional and actual do not always coincide. The danger is particularly acute in Visconti's case because of a peculiarity in his method of work which we first noticed in connection with *La Terra Trema*. In *Rocco and his Brothers*, as in *La Terra Trema*, he started with a clear intellectual conception of what he wanted to say, and then saw this conception gradually modify itself in response to suggestions that came to him as he worked. In *La Terra Trema* the result was almost a new film. In *Rocco and his Brothers* the effect is partly of enrichment and partly of confusion. Alterations were made to the script right up to the last minute. Then, during the shooting, scenes which had been restrained in intention were developed in a way which belies the original indications in the script. As a result changes have taken place in the structure of the film which Visconti perhaps did not fully foresee and which he would not necessarily recognise as having taken place.[3]

The general direction in which these changes work is to alter the balance between positive and negative characters. Those who gain in stature from the changes at the expense of the others are Rocco and the mother. Both of them in theory represent a backward form of consciousness of which the film set out to be a critique. But in their different ways they both of them achieve in practice a grandeur and a tragic quality which is denied to the others. Ciro, in particular, the next brother after Rocco, is overshadowed. His role, originally intended to be positive and important, is correspondingly reduced, and he appears as a shadowy and insignificant character whose main function seems to be to clear up the mess caused by the titanic struggle of the major figures.

Just how this shift in the balance came about is not easy to analyse. Partly it seems to be due to the acting, and to a potential discovered in the figurations when the film was under way. The imperious power and enormous egotism conveyed in Katina Paxinou's performance exceed any indications of the mother's character given in the script. In one sequence in particular, early on in the film, when she is trying to pack her sons off to work shovelling snow off the streets in the early morning, Visconti allows her total histrionic domination of the scene. Her possessiveness and ambition come across as a tremendous, loving, and all-embracing dynamism sweeping the family onwards towards the justice and success that are its rightful due. That her possessiveness is selfish and tyrannical and her ambitions pernicious and misplaced emerges as a mere abstract reflection by comparison with the sympathetic power of the performance.

Partly, however, even here, the shift can be seen as a necessary consequence of the translation of an intellectual conception into concrete images. At an immediate level, on the screen, there is no positive and negative, only real and unreal. The true significance of the mother's tyrannical behaviour has to be deciphered from a set of loose indications scattered throughout the film. There is no doubting her reality, but intuition (or prejudice) alone is not enough to enable one to see, from behind the performance, just what the mother is doing. For that one needs a grasp of the structure, and a structure which is pellucid enough in print may not be so when the script is turned into film. What particularly unbalances the contrast between Rocco and Ciro, in these terms, is that Rocco's role is defined in action throughout the film, and Ciro's mainly by a long speech which he delivers at the end. However evenly matched they might be on paper, translation into images was bound to disturb the balance.

The scaling down of the positive figure of Ciro had, however, begun earlier, during the elaboration of the final script. Visconti originally envisaged him as a trade-union militant, and clearly representative, from a Socialist viewpoint, of positive class consciousness. In the final script, as in the finished film, he is a more ordinary figure altogether—a lad who goes to night school and studies to get technical qualifications and to integrate himself as a skilled mechanic in the industrial world.

One last change should be mentioned in order to complete the picture, and that is the removal during the editing of an opening sequence dedicated to the mother and set in Lucania in Southern

Italy before the family's journey to Milan. In the literary structure this had a clear function, which was to situate the mother very emphatically in her peasant environment and to establish a point of reference against which her behaviour in Milan could be understood and eventually criticised. In the film as it stands the point is not entirely lost, but there is no doubt that dropping this scene means that the socially determined motivations in the figure of the mother are less clearly brought out than they would have been. Helped by Paxinou's performance she becomes more autonomous as a person. Anthropomorphism takes over from sociology, and in the process the film becomes much more ambivalent than a reading of the script would suggest.

This ambivalence is deeply rooted in the structure of the film, and has led to *Rocco and his Brothers* being interpreted in two apparently contradictory fashions, as a psychological drama and as a political tract. That it is not, even in intention and still less as finally realised, a simple political tract, can be demonstrated from the changes that Visconti made in the film as it proceded. But the other interpretation is equally fallacious. The political element derived from the scenario survives into the film. It does not act as the motor of the action, but provides a critical perspective necessary to judgment of the drama.

The story of *Rocco and his Brothers* unfolds as a series of episodes, merging into each other, in which each of Rosaria Pafundi's five sons moves in turn to occupy the centre of the stage. Each brother in a crude sense represents a certain kind of solution to the problems facing a Southern immigrant in a Northern urban environment. These solutions are not abstractly conceived, but evolve dialectically, each in response to the contradictions and inadequacies discovered in the last. The film opens with the bewildered arrival of Rosaria and four of her sons, Simone, Rocco, Ciro, and Luca, at the Stazione Centrale in Milan. The eldest son, Vincenzo, is already settled in the North and is engaged to the daughter of another immigrant family. It is in her house that the Pafundi find Vincenzo, and their arrival instantly sparks off a row between the two clans, with Vincenzo uneasily trapped between

his loyalty and submission to his family on the one hand, and his love for Ginetta and his determination to keep his independence on the other. Vincenzo has opted for an easy compromise: a steady if undemanding job and a wife from his own community to assist his integration. But Rosaria admits of no compromise where the family is concerned. She loses him his job and drives a wedge between him and the sophisticated, *petit-bourgeois* Ginetta, by imposing on him her conception of sexual relations in which the man, her son, should take himself a woman, if necessary by force. In an attempt to get Ginetta back, Vincenzo articulates these ideas to her and is smartly slapped in the face as a result. It is a long time before he and Ginetta and their respective families are again reconciled.

Vincenzo's mediocrity and confusion of loyalties does not escape Simone. His solution is more radical, but again it is limited by his roots, both moral and material, in the immigrant world. He asserts his independence of family ties, though he is prepared to profit from them whenever convenient. He becomes a boxer, which is a classic mode of advancement for ambitious members of exploited but emergent ethnic groups. He also starts going out with Nadia, a good-time girl who stands in the same relation to him as Ginetta does to Vincenzo. Also of immigrant descent, and also more emancipated intellectually than her man, her pursuit of the good life has led her to become a prostitute. Simone too sells his body for financial gain, both by becoming a boxer and also (an even more pointed parallel) by using his sexual attractiveness to seduce a middle-aged woman in order to steal her jewels.

The trouble that Simone gets into rebounds on to Rocco. Faced with Simone's excesses and gradual degeneration into criminality, Rocco, who after Simone was his mother's favourite, sees it as his responsibility to hold the family together, and sacrifices himself body and soul not only to Simone and the family but to the system that subjugates them. During his military service he encounters Nadia, just released from a spell inside, in one of those Italian provincial towns that seem to exist only for the sake of their barracks and their prison. He and Nadia fall in love. Simone is

both jealous and offended. As the elder brother he claims proprie-
tary right to Nadia, as his woman. He finds out that Rocco and
Nadia are together, and rapes her while two of his friends hold on
to Rocco and force him to be a passive and humiliated spectator of
what is going on. Simone then turns against Rocco, who hardly
defends himself, and beats him up.

When he has recovered Rocco finds Nadia again and tells her
that he can't be with her any more and that she should go back to
Simone. This perverse act of self-sacrifice, which Rocco makes as
they stand together on the pinnacled roof of Milan Cathedral, leads
also to Nadia's destruction. Simone is heavily in debt, and to rescue
him Rocco sells himself to the boxing promoter on a long-term
contract. Rocco is fundamentally incapable of hatred, either towards his brother or towards his opponents. For his brother's sake
he learns to be a boxer and to overcome his natural gentleness in
the ring. At the same time, however, Simone's violence to Nadia
has penetrated below the defences of Rocco's ideological non-
violence. Though he still refuses to hate his brother openly or to
admit the ambivalence of his feelings, there is an element of
repressed hatred for Simone, as well as of self-sacrifice, that now
drives him on in the ring.

One evening, when Rocco is fighting, Simone finds Nadia, whom
he had brought to live with him in his mother's flat, and who had
left after a row with Rosaria, and he takes her out into the country.
The barrier of communication between them is total. In a final
attempt to break through to her, he assaults her, then desists in
horror at his own violence. She is ice-cold and resigned. She wants
nothing from him except an end to the misery he has caused her.
When he advances towards her with a knife, she lifts her arms
from her sides in a gesture of crucifixion. He stabs her once without
emotion, then paroxysmically again and again.[4] Meanwhile, in
parallel montage, Rocco is shown fighting for his life against a
stronger and fiercer opponent. With his guard wide open and blood
on his face he seems to be going under, then appears to remember
himself and what he is supposed to be doing there. With a last
effort he summons up all the savagery he is capable of feeling and

Rocco and his Brothers: Rocco and Nadia

pursues his opponent round the ring and knocks him down. While Simone walks away, alone, from Nadia's body, family and friends crowd jubilantly round Rocco in celebration of his success.

The contrasts contained in the montage between Simone's murder of Nadia and Rocco's symbolic slaughter of his opponent are of various kinds. At the most basic and generalised level there is the counterpointing of two forms of violence. In terms of the relationship between the brothers there is a reference to Rocco's sacrifice of himself to Simone, and the fruitless and indeed catastrophic result of this sacrifice. Within Rocco's own psychological development there is the fact that he has learnt to hate. There is also in Rocco's determination, an implied contrast with Simone's own career as a boxer. Simone was very good at demolishing weaker opponents, but easily collapsed under pressure. His response to his predicament with Nadia is in a sense predicated in his career as a boxer, both in the fact that it was in the ring that he acquired the habit of violence, and in his bafflement when faced with a situation which he cannot easily dominate. Finally, there is in the scene a purely rhythmic parallelism between the two events, the two acts of revenge—Simone's against Nadia and Rocco's against his destiny of sacrifice—which are both equally tragic and absurd, and which achieve their climax at the same time.

The tragic destinies of Simone and Rocco effectively end here, with this sequence, which is the dramatic high-point of the film. The next phase belongs to Ciro. Simone appears, bloodstained, at the family party where Rocco's victory is being celebrated. Rocco and the mother, for Simone's sake and that of the family, take him in and prepare to shield him. But Ciro escapes from the party and denounces Simone to the police. For a long time he has watched with dismay the narrow loyalties and extreme solidarity of the family group. Now the time has come when he finds himself obliged to act, and does so ruthlessly, opening up the family sanctum to the cold winds of external justice.

In a final sequence Ciro explains to Luca, the youngest brother, what he has done and why he did it. Luca is still a child, and his horizons are bounded by the family. Unlike the others he remembers the South only vaguely, but he has the idea that he would like some day to go back, to renew contact with the world of his origins. Ciro has no such nostalgia. He has fought hard to liberate himself from the burden of being a Southerner, and has no intention of sacrificing his hard-won gains; his Milanese girl-friend, his skilled job at Alfa Romeo. By betraying his family he has broken the last remaining tie with the past. Luca, who is so much younger, will be able to enjoy the luxury of rediscovering his roots: Ciro cannot.

The final dialogue completes the process whereby the initiative is passed from one brother to the next and we are given an insight into the problem facing each one and the way each reacts against the last and carries on from where his elder brother left off. But by the time we reach the end the procedure has become summary and intellectualised. Ciro and Luca, compared with Simone and Rocco, are mere symbols. They articulate (Luca childishly, Ciro in a more adult fashion) their own consciousness of who they are and what they have to do. The story ends with them, as a formality: the drama has already ended.

It would be truer to say, however, that the continuity from Simone to Rocco to Ciro to Luca is a hangover from the literary structure with which Visconti started. The significance of the changes in the shape of the film which we analysed above lies here, in the qualitative difference they created between Rosaria, Simone, and Rocco on the one hand, and Ciro and Luca on the other. The tragedy of destruction involves the first three only. Ciro and Luca are not participants. From the start of the film they are cast in the role of observers, and they survive to assimilate the lesson of the past and to carry on into the future.

Luca is a pure symbol, representing the future, and comparable, in Visconti's work, to the child that 'Ntoni talks to at the end of *La Terra Trema*. Ciro is more complex. Like Pietro in *Vaghe Stelle dell'Orsa*, he is an inheritor. What gives him his freedom is the destruction of the family. But unlike Pietro he is also a member of the family and is responsible for consummating its destruction when he denounces Simone to the police. Up to that moment, however, his role in the drama had been insignificant, and even the

Rocco and his Brothers: Ciro and his girl-friend →

act of denunciation falls outside the family drama proper. He is also unlike the other members of the family in that from the outset he manages to go his own way. He is determined to carve himself out a future in his new environment, and involves himself as little as possible in family affairs. Whereas Rocco takes up the burden of Simone's sins on the family's behalf, Ciro feels no such obligations. All he gets from the family is a roof over his head and a knowledge of what not to be, and how to avoid the disaster that is in store.

In relation to the family, therefore, Ciro's role is that of a detached consciousness. The life he participates in is elsewhere, in the outside world. His denunciation of Simone brings the two worlds together. Over and above his role in the family structure he represents a new social type altogether. He is the first of the brothers to integrate successfully into Northern society. His conceptions are those of a Northern industrial worker and no longer those inherited from his peasant family. It is in accordance with these conceptions that he is able to denounce his brother, and in so doing save the family from itself.

For what destroys the family is not Ciro's action but its own extraordinary internal loyalties and the contradiction between these and the society in which it finds itself. Rosaria, Rocco, and Simone are all victims of a conception of the family which has no relevance whatever to life in an industrial society. To Rosaria, Simone's murder of Nadia is a *delitto d'onore*, a just vengeance for her "infidelity". Like the Austrian general in *Senso* who finds Livia's denunciation of Franz more reprehensible than Franz's desertion, Rosaria has a moral code in terms of which Ciro is guilty of a gross betrayal in comparison with which Simone's crime is of no significance. Rocco's appreciation of the situation is similar to his mother's, but is couched in more individualistic and religious terms. His feeling towards Simone is of personal as well as family loyalty. If he gives up Nadia to Simone partly because Simone has a right to her decreed by custom, it is also because his whole ideology is one of sacrifice. He loves Simone and will do anything for him. He refuses to denounce him to "the justice of men", and his own conception of justice involves taking upon himself,

Christ-like, the burden of the sins of the world. As Ciro points out, Rocco is a saint, and his saintliness is as irrelevant and as disastrous as Rosaria's belief in the family and Simone's criminality.

The criminal Simone is in many ways the most interesting character of all. He has two assets to help him escape his sub-proletarian destiny, his sexual charm and his strength, and he uses them to the full. When they run out he has nothing else to rely on. He tries to have things all ways, to enjoy Nadia for what she is and to possess her as of right in accordance with his primitive mascu-linist ideas. What he lacks is a knowledge of his own limits, and the capacity to gauge the extent of his corruption and the precarious nature of his conquests. Ciro's judgment of him, as a source of corruption poisoning the whole rest of the family, is unduly harsh. Simone is corrupted by society more than he himself corrupts. He is permanently childlike. He is accustomed to getting all he can have, and in a world where there is so much more to be got he wants all that as well.

The source of corruption, in so far as it can be made particular, is Nadia. She has a much clearer idea than does Simone of the limits of what she can expect, and unlike Simone she is completely emancipated from traditional conceptions of sexual morality. To her Simone is a man of a certain type, with whom she can have a certain kind of relationship, and Rocco is another. To Simone, however, Nadia can only be a prostitute or a wife. When she refuses to be either he breaks down completely. Until it is too late she miscalculates the strength of his passion and the extent to which he holds her responsible for his failure. With Rocco she hopes to find a man who makes no claims for possession and to whom she does not prostitute herself either, and again she mis-calculates, not because of anything in Rocco as a person but because of his relationship with Simone. Neither man is in a position to supply what she is looking for.

Rocco and his Brothers is not an entirely satisfactory film. It is really two films in one, an epic and a drama. The epic concerns the journey of the Pafundi family to the North of Italy, its gradual conquest of a future in its new environment, and the liberation of

Ciro from Rosaria. The drama is the story of the triangle Simone-Nadia-Rocco, of Rocco's self-sacrifice and Simone's murder of Nadia. As heroes, Rocco and Ciro are in no way comparable. They stand for the two different ways in which the film has been interpreted, the drama and the tract. Rocco's crises, his suffering and sacrifice, make him a tragic and dramatic figure who engages our sympathies at an emotional level. But once the drama has run its course the more intellectual vision reasserts itself. Ciro, who as a character is insignificant but whose historical role is far more important, emerges to put Rocco's tragedy into perspective. The two do not contradict each other. Rocco's tragedy is no less real for being forced on him by a conception of the world which is subsequently criticised. But nor does it annul the criticism.

To a certain extent, as we have seen, this central ambiguity is allowed for in the construction of the film. The epic and the drama overlap and are deliberately counterpointed. The individual and the historical are set up in conflict with each other, and the outcome of the conflict is that the individual is defeated. But it is not possible to see either the conflict or its resolution as directly or exclusively representative of Visconti's conscious intentions. The ambiguity does not lie simply in the problem that is posed, and left unanswered, in *Rocco and his Brothers*. It strikes deeper and reflects a constant tension in Visconti's work between an intellectual belief in the cause of progress and an emotional nostalgia for the past world that is being destroyed. A comparison between the finished films and their original scenarios, not only in the case of *Rocco and his Brothers*, shows up the dichotomy clearly. On the level of intentions all Visconti's historical films—*La Terra Trema, Senso, Rocco and his Brothers, The Leopard,* and *Vaghe Stelle dell'Orsa*—can be read as an illustration of a conception of history in which change is both welcome and inevitable. But in the final realisation nostalgia prevails over progress. The individual—Franz, Rocco, the Prince, Gianni—rises to confront history and to be tragically defeated. Only in two films is this pattern contradicted. In *La Terra Trema* the defeated individual, 'Ntoni, is also the representative of progress and historical advance. In *White Nights* nostalgia, in the person of Natalia, comes out triumphant. These two films are limiting cases of a conception of the world which is consistent in its opposition of two conflicting ideals, one rooted emotionally in the past, and the other projected intellectually into the future. If we have chosen to finish on a study of *Rocco and his Brothers*, it is because it is here that this particular conflict, which is the problematic centre of all Visconti's work, is most explicitly expressed.

The sources of the conflict could be, and indeed have been,[5] traced to the anomaly of Visconti's position as both an aristocrat, living off a past heritage, and a Marxist and a Communist, committed to a belief in the Socialist future. But the question is not one of giving an explanation, in any case inadequate, of why the conflict should exist. It is more important to trace, within the films, the way the conflict is expressed and, if possible, resolved. As I have tried to show, the structure of Visconti's films is complex and often equivocal. Above all, the films are works of art. They reveal the world in a particular guise: not, perhaps, how it *is* in an objective sense; nor, for that matter, necessarily how we would like it to be; but how it can be perceived and experienced by a particular individual at a particular time.

NOTES

1. Originally as far back as 1943 ("Il Cinema Antropomorfico" in *Cinema*, first series, no. 173–4).
2. Post-synchronising is normal practice in Italy even when the actors are native Italian speakers, and the technique has been developed to a fine art.
3. Visconti's own explanation of the changes that take place during the making of a film is by an analogy, borrowed from Renoir, between cinema and ceramics (see his introduction to the script of *Vaghe Stelle dell'Orsa*, Capelli).
4. The repeated stabbing has been cut by the British censor, with the perverse result that the murder is more horrible than in the original, because it looks premeditated and cold-blooded which in reality it is not.
5. For an interpretation of Visconti which revolves largely round this anomaly of his personal position see Yves Guillaume, *Visconti* (Paris, Editions Universitaires, 1966).

10: Lo Straniero, The Damned, Death in Venice

After *Vaghe Stelle dell'Orsa* Visconti was contracted to make an episode for *Le Streghe*, a Dino De Laurentiis production starring the still incomparable Silvana Mangano. It was an insignificant moment in his career, and was to be followed by an even worse one —his film adaptation of Camus' *L'Etranger*. It was depressingly evident, as soon as the project was announced, that as an adaptation the film was unlikely to be a success: the only hope was that Visconti, by a suitably arrogant disregard for the letter of the text, might yet succeed in creating a film, loosely inspired by the events recounted by Camus, that could stand on its own without need for reference to the original. Any such hopes were soon disappointed. *Lo Straniero*, to give the film its Italian title, is a literal and even pedantic adaptation, and a film which it would be better to be able to forget were it not for the fact that its failure is symptomatic of the involution of its author's concern.

The crucial and irredeemable weakness of the film lies in its subservience to a quite fictitious notion of "great" literature, important because it is great and worthy of obeisance rather than because it has certain specific (and specifically literary) qualities. With age Visconti's subservience to the monuments of literary culture has steadily increased, first of all in his theatrical and operatic work and now in his films. A brief survey of his career serves to show how the process has gradually intensified over the years. In his early work there is almost always a pre-existing literary text somewhere in the background, but it serves as a starting-point and not as a point of arrival. Thus *Ossessione* is derived from James Cain's thriller, *The Postman always Rings Twice*; *La Terra Trema* adopts a plot structure based on that of Verga's *I Malavoglia*; *Senso* comes from a "novella" of the same title by Camillo Boito and *White Nights* from Dostoievsky. But in none of these works is the film put forward as in any way the equivalent of the novel. In *Ossessione* the setting is changed and the action simplified. In *La Terra Trema* Verga's "style indirect libre" is replaced by a deliberate effect of distanciation, the action is updated and the political lesson reversed, so that Verga's metaphysical fatalism is repudiated both in the style and in the ostensive political content. In *Senso* the modifications take one even further from the character of the original text. Not only is the narrative filled out with all sorts of new detail, but the mode of narration is changed so that nothing survives to link the novella and the film except a basic situation and the outline of a plot.[1] *White Nights*, which follows, is perhaps closer to its original than any of the previous films, but even there it is clear that the function of the adaptation has been to produce a new work which uses the literary original as a suggestive source of ideas and structures. As for the supposed derivation of *Rocco and his Brothers* from Thomas Mann's monumental *Joseph and his Brethren*, this is little more than an act of homage expressed in the similarity of the titles, while the adaptation of part of the narrative from Testori's play *Il ponte della Ghisolfa*, though less fictitious, is still insignificant.

In the 1960s, however, the pattern changes. Of Visconti's films since *Rocco* (excluding the recently finished *Ludwig*) two are made from what at first look like original scripts and three are literal adaptations of literary classics. Of the original scripts that of *Vaghe Stelle dell'Orsa* can claim a vague literary antecedent in Aeschylus' 'Oresteia' and that of *The Damned* can lay an equally tenuous claim to a Shakespearian origin, basically Macbeth, but with a little Hamlet thrown in, together with a bit from Visconti's great culture heroes, Dostoievsky and Mann. What has in fact happened is that these generic cultural derivations have taken the place previously occupied by a particular novel or short story. They pin the film to something already existing—in the world of culture if not in the world that is the eventual subject of the film—but theoretically at least they leave the author of the film free to develop his material stylistically in an original way. In practice, however, the extended metaphors which they invoke act as a surrogate for original development according to the inner necessity of the material. Far more than in the early loose adaptations the film threatens to become a discourse on culture and on the permanence of myth rather than an authentic representation of actual events. In *La Terra Trema* the Verga text remains in the background. It makes an interesting point of comparison for evaluating the significance of the film, but it is not part of the intended meaning. In *The Damned*, on the other hand, and even, to a lesser extent, in *Vaghe Stelle*, there is no text, absent or present, to which one is referred, but there is a myth, and the myth remains forcibly in the foreground because of the way it is overlaid on the events.

With the other three films it is not just a myth or a series of cultural references which assume this foreground presence but the text itself. In each case the adaptation is literal in intention and the work adapted is one which enjoys a reputation as a classic, Tomasi di Lampedusa's *The Leopard*, Camus' *L'Etranger* and Mann's *Death in Venice*. The texts are not chosen in order to be subsequently forgotten once they have served their purpose of providing material for the movie, but on the contrary in order to be remembered. Though the films can be read naïvely, without reference to the literary originals, this is clearly not the author's intention, which is rather to produce, for the cinema, an instant equivalent of a literary classic. The film is "the film of the book" and it arrogates to itself the merit of the book as one of the reasons for seeing it. Not only that, but it is intrinsic to the meaning of the film that it be seen as referring to a known original, situating it and adding its own meaning in the form of interpretation. Thus, with *The Leopard* Visconti is presenting not so much a story from the history of the Risorgimento as Lampedusa's reflections on the Risorgimento further reflected on and corrected by Luchino Visconti.

Now there is an essential difference between the adaptation of *The Leopard* and the other two, which is that in the former case Visconti can refer behind the text to a history of real events of which his representation and Lampedusa's can be seen as alternative and equally valid transcriptions. Lampedusa's novel belongs in the tradition of realistic literature which refers to and reflects, in the form of an action, a content of real characters or real events seen as prior to and distinct from their literary elaboration. But because, in realistic art generally and in the historical novel in particular, the reality referred to possesses this ontological priority over the representation subsequently made of it, it follows that the author of a particular representation has no exclusive monopoly on the events shown. It is quite possible for the author to be inaccurate or "wrong" in attributing certain thoughts or actions to his characters and for another author, faced with the same real material, to produce a representation which is "better" or more accurate, based on a superior historical interpretation of the content of the events. This is the procedure adopted by Visconti in *The Leopard*. The two works, novel and film, differ, not only by being in different media, but in offering different and alternative versions of the same reality. Thus, if in the Visconti the story is more public, more obviously linked to the macroscopic events of world history, this is not so much a product of the intrinsic objectivity of the film medium as a specifically different interpretation, by Visconti, of events which Lampedusa chose to describe in a more personalistic and microscopic way.

For this to be possible two conditions are necessary. First it applies only to avowedly realist works, and secondly it implies a theory of realism which puts forward the referential character of the work as in fact paramount. This naïve conception of realism is, however, implausible, to put it mildly. Flaubert's *Madame Bovary*, for example, is held up as a model of realism, but it is clear that in relation to the novel one cannot separate a real Yonville l'Abbaye or a real Emma Bovary from the specific representation of them which is contained in Flaubert's style and there alone. It is significant that the most famous film adaptations of *Madame Bovary*, by

Renoir and by Minnelli, are both *films d'auteur* in which the representation is in no way reducible to a common content but is in the first instance characteristic of the two very different directors who have chosen the novel as a starting-point for their films. But if this is already the case with realist works themselves, it is so even more for those works, particularly twentieth-century, where the referential element is minimal and the character of the work is defined entirely by the mode of representation—or, to put it more strongly, where events only exist in so far as they are the object of representation on the part of the author.

It is hard to think of a more extreme case of this than Camus' "récit" (it is not even a novel) *L'Etranger*. A man, a *pied noir* living in Algiers, hears the news of his mother's death in a home out in the country; he goes to her funeral; on his return he makes it with a girl he has met on the beach; while visiting a friend he points a revolver at and shoots dead an Arab who in a vague way is threatening his friend; he is arrested and condemned to death for murder. This action does not cohere as a plot but merely as a possible succession of events, and the significance of the events, in so far as they are significant, lies in their discontinuity, and, to a lesser extent, in the attempt by the court trying the case to impose a continuity upon them and find ordered motivation where none exists. But while the writing hints at various possibilities of interpretation— psychological, sociological or whatever—it does so only to deny them and to withdraw instantly into a perfect narrative neutrality. Not for nothing did Roland Barthes in *Le Degré zéro de l'écriture* define Camus' style in *L'Etranger* as representing not a presence but an absence—"la façon d'exister d'un silence".[2]

There are various ways in which this silence could be treated in a film. One would be to respect it, after the fashion, say, of Peter Brook's film of *Moderato Cantabile*, and to develop a kind of cinematic "écriture blanche" equivalent to that of the book. Another would be to disregard it entirely and construct the film not around Camus' style but around the content which the style fleetingly suggests. Alternatively the book could be torn apart and the emptiness at the centre which is both its charm and its limit shown up as an ideological flight from the reality of the colonial world. Visconti is hardly the most plausible director for the first of these options, since his style is anything but silent and could indeed be summed up as essentially noisy. As between the other two he appears, on a charitable hypothesis, to have chosen a compromise. There is some evidence[3] that he at least flirted with the third option and that the gross realism of much of *Lo Straniero* derives from an attempt to realise materially, through the film, the structure of relationships of which the consciousness of the hero, Meursault, provides a distorted reflection. Certainly since the Algerian revolution it has become commonplace to subject Camus' work to a political critique on broadly Fanonist lines, bringing out the impossibility for a colonialist writer (which Camus was, though he was other things besides) of coping actively and in a non-mystified way with the reality of the colonial situation. To do this in a film would be extremely difficult, since it would involve extricating the different roles of the author, Camus, and of Meursault as both narrator and protagonist, and then relating these dialectically to the various aspects of the reality of colonial Algiers. In the last analysis all that Visconti succeeds in doing, apart from presenting the text as in some mysterious way important, is to use the camera to "realise" the events to which the text makes reference and to crowd out the silence with a host of unnecessary and obtrusive presences. The film becomes a murder story in which there is no enigma beyond that of a sad man (played in most typical fashion by Marcello Mastroianni) who commits a meaningless crime in a moment of bewilderment and confusion and is then pursued by all the panoply of bourgeois justice. The generic realism to which the narrative is subjected is enriched in certain scenes, such as those in the courtroom, by the use of flashy melodramatic emphases, and the film ends with the formerly pathetic central character metamorphosed into titanic hero as he proudly refuses the ministrations of the Church and prepares to go to his death alone. Against this travesty of the original, which in fact neither respects the original nor seriously criticises it, there are to be set a number of moments which have a distinctive and surprising quality of their own, owing nothing to Camus. The scenes with the old people from the home and in particular one sequence of shots of an old man following the coffin have a directness and an authenticity at the simplest level of constructive observation which is the more remarkable since they have no parallel in Visconti's own work since *Ossessione*, a quarter of a century earlier—almost as if the characters from the earlier film had been brought out of retirement for the purpose. It also occasionally happens, though it is not clear whether by accident or design, that at moments the text is prised away from Camus and from the portentous narration of its "existential" hero and achieves effects of a brute physicality of existence which are, ironically, closer to the sense of the original than all the attempts to follow the verbal form of the *récit*. At these moments the film actually begins to make sense, because the spectator is made aware of the gap between the existentialist consciousness and the world it aspires but fails to comprehend. But they are few and far between, and in any case contradict the approach of the rest of the film, which is to fill in the gaps with "realistic" tittle-tattle.

With *The Damned* we re-enter familiar Visconti territory. It is a story, like *Vaghe Stelle* and *La Terra Trema*, of the decline and decomposition of a family, but, as in *Senso* and *The Leopard*, the fortunes of individuals are linked to wider developments at a climactic moment of history. Like the House of Salina in *The Leopard*, the Essenbeck family are, willingly or not, historical protagonists. As one of the "grandes familles" of pre-war German capitalism, their private destinies cannot be separated from those of the State, and the rise of Nazism involves them both in political accommodations and in personal disintegration.

The plot is complex. The head of the family, Joachim, is due to retire. His eventual heir is his grandson Martin, but he has two possible immediate inheritors, Herbert who is a liberal and an anti-Fascist and Konstantin, a Nazi fanatic and member of the S.A. His temperamental choice, Herbert, has to be sacrificed, but, to control the possible excesses of Konstantin, an outsider to the family, Friedrich Bruckmann, is made managing director of the steel works. Friedrich is also the lover of Sophie, mother of the decadent Martin who is generally judged unsuitable but will in any case formally inherit when he comes of age. Friedrich is backed by Aschenbach, a cousin of the family who is in the S.S. and has his own reasons for opposing Konstantin. In the end Friedrich comes within an ace of getting what he wants, marriage to Sophie and control of the firm, but meanwhile the S.S. have switched their allegiance and with their help Martin is able to outmanoeuvre Friedrich and force him and Sophie to commit suicide on the very day of their marriage.

Such is the background to the plot. The foreground action is concentrated in a few key sequences, of which the most important are those of Joachim's birthday party and retirement, which coincides with the burning of the Reichstag; the elimination of Konstantin during the Night of the Long Knives; and the marriage and death of Sophie and Friedrich, which also represents the total Nazification of the surviving Von Essenbeck house. Of these sequences that of the Night of the Long Knives is most often cited as a *tour de force*, which it indeed is. What is more interesting, though, than the overlong and overdecorative staging of the S.A. orgy, is the way Visconti represents the relationship between the Nazism of the S.A. and that of the S.S. Rejecting the Brechtian analogy of two gangs of hoods fighting a private war for control of the rackets, he makes a sharp distinction between the mob fascism of the S.A. squads and the efficient militarism of the S.S., identified with the New Order and with the Nazi state itself. The brown-shirts, favoured instruments of counter-revolutionary violence during the rise of fascism and expression of reactionary populism up to the time of the seizure of power, have served their purpose. Unattractive though they are, even in their moments of *Kameradschaft* and relaxation, there is something pathetic about their elimination by the disciplined and well-armed agents of state power. As they lounge around and drink their beer and sing their Teutonic songs, the lake on whose shore they have held their rally is gradually surrounded by motorised units of S.S. In the ensuing massacre Friedrich personally dispatches the coarse and cretinous Konstantin, but there is more to it than that. Populist fascism has been destroyed, and the new state order, fusing Party, Capital and military High Command, is firmly established.

Less emphatic, but more subtle, are the scenes at the beginning of the film, again involving both a major political turning-point and another murder committed by the ambitious Friedrich. Whereas in the Long Knives sequence the relationship between the private and political is represented only by the somewhat arbitrary presence of Friedrich at the massacre, a presence motivated only by a suggestion from the S.S. man Aschenbach that Friedrich should give concrete proof of his loyalty, here the threads are more closely intertwined. Friedrich murders Joachim, at the same time persuading the anti-Fascist Herbert to escape the country, thus making his political flight seem like a confession to the murder. Meanwhile Joachim's party has been the setting in which other complexities of family divisions have been presented, and a rather cheap bit of montage connects a revelation of Martin's penchant for little girls with the murder of the old man. As Martin makes his advance to one of the younger children there is a scream, which is not her cry of shock but the opening of the next sequence with the discovery of Joachim's body.[4]

Paedophilia is not the only pathological tendency to which Martin inclines. While in the entertainment for Joachim his cousin Günther treats the company to a spot of unaccompanied Bach on the cello and the younger children under the direction of their French governess recite a poem in Italian, Martin's contribution to the proceedings is a cabaret song in drag, "Einen Mann, einen richtigen Mann", expressing in passing a typically Viscontian contrast between traditional "culture" and modern "barbarism". More important, Martin is in love with his mother. She trades on this, encouraging his erotic dependence as far as possible, but at a crucial moment she goes too far. Wishing to gain his consent for her marriage to Friedrich she starts to seduce him, but the seduction turns into a rape of the mother by the son, leaving Martin triumphant and Sophie humiliated and on the verge of madness. It is this act, combined with Sophie's failure to hold together the alliance of

Friedrich and Aschenbach, which leads to her and Friedrich's isolation and death. The defection of Konstantin's son Günther from Bach-playing intellectual and sympathiser with Herbert to fully-fledged Nazi is all that is needed to consummate the process.

Stylistically the film is, for the most part, classically Viscontian, notably in its operatic articulation into scenes between the protagonists and scenes with chorus. Particularly fine, because realised with a surprising economy of means, is the 'duet' in the state files between Sophie and Aschenbach which provides the first intimations of Friedrich's impending fall. Here the absence of sumptuous or splendid décors is more expressive than their presence would have been, for the anonymous bureaucratism of the setting counterpoints the heroics of the characters and exposes their limitations. All too often in the film, however, the rather stagy settings threaten to take control of the action which is being played out in front of them. In *Senso* and in *Vaghe Stelle* the two elements were held in dynamic equilibrium. Here the dynamism begins to fade and it is as if the set were threatening to cave in and swamp the characters in its ruin. This is particularly noticeable at the end, when the plot has, so to speak, run out. Heightened naturalism shades into expressionism. The characters, having lost their autonomy, become masks, and what began as tragedy ends as grotesque.[5]

In general, then, *The Damned* is a confident, if not entirely successful, return to the operatic-melodramatic mode which first appears with *La Terra Trema* and carries on through to *Vaghe Stelle*. But there are differences. On the one hand there are scenes in which the melodramatic elements are dropped in favour of a simpler form of iconic realism, lucid and easy to read but dense with symbolic overtones. Such for example is the scene of Joachim's funeral, with the procession winding its way slowly through dingy streets past the Essenbeck steelworks. Here the symbolism is associative, pointing directly to a material reality of socio-economic relations without passing through the mediation of character and drama. It is not a scene which either in its conception or in its detail could have come from the camera of a Minnelli or a Sirk and is a reminder of Visconti's past links with neo-realism and the realist tradition in general. But there are on the other hand also scenes in which the movement away from the self-contained universe of melodrama takes an opposing direction, and one which is not at all easy to define.

The stylistic indicator of this change of direction is given by the descent into expressionism most apparent at the end of the film. Visconti's melodrama most often has the form of anthropomorphic historicism, that is to say the movement of social forces is reflected in the actions and passions of individuals expressed through the representation of character. *The Damned*, like *Senso* or *The Leopard* is a character drama, but character is not inexhaustible as a source of artistic representation. The political criticism levelled against *The Damned* that the history of Nazism is after all not the same as the history of German capitalism, let alone one capitalist family, is irrelevant in general, since *The Damned* does not aspire to be a history of Nazism. But it is correct in one particular, which is that the Nazi phenomenon exceeds in horror what any one family can do to itself. In *The Damned* the family is self-destroyed, under the pressure of Nazism. But what has happened to Germany is worse, and cannot be represented, except obliquely. Of course things can be referred to, and we learn for example that Herbert's wife, Elisabeth, has died in Dachau. But, at a level of direct representation, Martin's assumption of S.S. uniform and the chilly mask-like face of Sophie at the moment of her marriage and forced suicide are as symbols both extreme and yet inadequate. The characters, as characters, have become irrelevant, but their value as emblems of social forces has been undermined and the film ends on a void, expressionism with nothing to express.

It is instructive to compare the closing sequence of *The Damned* with that of *Vaghe Stelle*, both for the recurrence of the same image —the mother transfixed in quasi-catatonic madness—and for the sense of an ending on to total emptiness. But whereas in *Vaghe Stelle*, which is a true melodrama, the emptiness marks the completion of a cycle of events according to the pattern of a unitary myth, that of the Oresteia, in the case of *The Damned* there is no proper conclusion on any level. Historically the moment chosen is not important; in terms of psychological drama Friedrich, though out-manoeuvred, has not been internally destroyed, while the under-lying mythic structure has not been strong enough to impose the ending as a formal necessity. All the time the film has operated, covertly, on the three levels of history, drama and myth. The end comes when these three threads are arbitrarily snapped.

The simplest explanation of what has happened would be to say that Visconti has bitten off more than he could chew, and that the film suffers, as did *Rocco and his Brothers*, basically from an excess of ambition. This is true up to a point, but it is interesting only if one can specify the precise way in which the film fails, in the last analysis, to achieve its ends. The key factor here is the introduction of the mythic element, which in *Rocco* is hardly present and appears for the first time in Visconti's work, very successfully, in *Vaghe Stelle*. In *The Damned* however, unlike in *Vaghe Stelle*, the myth element is neither unitary nor fully integrated into the structure of the narrative. It seems to have two functions, one as an external referent, and the second as an expedient designed to stop the film from falling apart. At the second level it is simply a failure. Friedrich and Sophie in the roles of Macbeth and Lady Macbeth would make sense on its own, as would the triangle Martin–Sophie–Friedrich as Hamlet–Gertrude–Claudius. But taken together they are merely a further source of confusion. While in the Oresteia the motives of political ambition and sexual jealousy are perfectly fused in one linear narrative, the Shakespearian sources are distinct. They offer the possibility of an association ambition–barbarism (*Macbeth*) and of another jealousy–corruption (*Hamlet*), both of which Visconti uses to the full, but no formal means to relate the two.

This leads us back to the notion of myth as external referent. Though formally ineffective, the myths are an important part of the content of the film. Over and above what is directly stated in the film itself, they imply a whole series of further statements about the permanence of certain driving forces in history and the trans-historical ineluctability of the tragic mechanism. As such they are not merely an expedient but a falsification, and it is not surprising if history, having found its first form of representation in tragedy, finds its repetition in grotesque. Not just Shakespeare but also Wagner (the original title of the film was *Götterdämmerung*, echoed in the Italian *La Caduta degli Dei*) is invoked to add overtones of monumentality to the story, though to no purpose. In the last analysis the Essenbecks are only the Essenbecks, more interesting to the world, perhaps, than the average family, because of the power of their capital; but their fall (only to rise again, without a doubt, in 1945) is neither the end of civilisation nor its restoration.

And yet, for the film, the Essenbecks are important. Not just as individuals, nor even for the economic force they represent, but precisely as *civilisation*. Just as the House of Salina represented Sicily, so they represent Germany. The peculiar philoaristocratic aberration of the "Marxist" Visconti is reinforced in *The Damned* by the influence in tandem of the honest bourgeois Thomas Mann and of the honest broker of Marxism and the bourgeois tradition, György Lukács. There is nothing surprising in this, since in the fifties (e.g. in *Senso*) Visconti was already using Lukácsian schemas of interpretation and applying them as a leftist camouflage to his own concern with decadentism, while his interest in Mann first emerges about the same time with the scenario of a ballet derived from the novella *Marius and the Magician* (1956).

It is not until *The Damned*, however, that this interest emerges as a kind of autonomous substitute for the Marxism to which Visconti formally subscribes. Strictly speaking Visconti has never (except perhaps at the time of *La Terra Trema*) been a Marxist director in the full sense of applying historical materialism and the materialist dialectic consistently throughout his film-making practice. Rather he has been a realist, but one who has used a Marxist-inspired view of history as an element in his films. This element is overlaid on the basic structure, in the form of an internal invitation, usually issued by one of the characters, to "read" the structure in Marxist terms. But the style remains basically that of nineteenth-century realism, in its melodramatic variant, so that the Marxist reading has the role of a correction and a critique of the basic material. *Senso*, for example, manages to be both a historical drama and a Marxist (or rather Lukácsian) interpretation of it rolled into one. So too is *The Leopard*, where the process is made more transparent by the fact that the film is an adaptation, in a Marxist or *marxisant* key of an originally non-Marxist text. The would-be Marxist critic has only to follow Visconti's discourse, at the anthropomorphic level and at that of the overlay (or implicit critique) in order to reach what can pass as an historical materialist interpretation of the content of the film. In *The Damned*, however, the overlay is Marxist only in the most perfunctory way,[6] and the reading which is integral to the film is one provided not by historical materialism but by a restatement of the values of European humanism. By a pardonable but nevertheless disturbing sleight of hand, these values are passed off, as they often are in Lukács, as providing the substance of a critique.

As a state of affairs there is nothing remarkable in this. Of what great directors in the realist tradition in the Western cinema can it be said that their representation of the world involves an historical materialist perspective which is openly and explicitly theirs rather than something used by a critic to explain the significance of what they are saying? Losey, perhaps: but Stroheim, Renoir, Preminger? What is interesting in Visconti's case is the process by which the critical content of his films has become progressively attenuated in a director who operates in a predominantly Marxist cultural context and who would still, I imagine, see himself as actively contributing to that culture. The key to the process, in my opinion, lies in the ambiguity of the Lukácsian concept of critical realism when used, not as part of a schema of interpretation but as a model for practice. The essence of critical realism lies in the possibility of putting into action a dual critique, first on the part of the author and then, subsequently, on the part of the critic proper. The author views bourgeois society from the inside, but without identification. He is both of it and not of it. While he shares the situation of his subject-matter his consciousness acts freely and critically in relation to it so that his writing offers a criticism as well as a reflection of the material presented to him. At a second stage, however, the true significance of the author's relationship with his material, the extent to which he comprehended the movement of which he was a part and the structural limitations to which he was subject as part of that movement, require in their turn to be analysed, and the function of Marxist historicist criticism is to provide such a retrospective analysis. The problem which arises for the Marxist artist who sees himself as operating in the critical realist mode is simply this. Given the necessity of a Marxist critique of the work, can he himself double up in the role of critic? The answer, unfortunately, is that he can not.[7]

It is a feature of Italian cultural life that it is often demanded of an artist that he should possess, as it were, a Marxian super-ego and that he should be able to justify himself and his activity in terms of what is, all said and done, a very inadequate theory of artistic practice, the theory of critical realism. Visconti's subterfuge consists in passing off his concern with culture in the guise of a critique, instead of confronting it for what it is: the raw material out of which he can fashion his own art. One of the great merits of *Vaghe Stelle dell'Orsa* is that it treats its own cultural problematic as primary artistic material. It is a realistic film only in so far as this problematic is real—real for the film's protagonists, for Visconti and for us as spectators. Because it has no pretensions to realism in the vulgar sense it also does not need (and certainly doesn't have) the kind of phoney "critical" super-ego approved by the "left" establishment. Partly as a consequence of this happy deficiency it did not receive a very favourable critical reception. All the pressure on Visconti was to return to procedures whose interest he had long since exhausted. The result, after the fiasco of *Lo Straniero*, was *The Damned*.

The failure of *Lo straniero*, compared with the relative success of *The Damned*, points, however, to another contradiction. It seems that Visconti's focus of interest in recent years has shifted from history as such, in the sense of a set of given events of which people are the agents, to culture in the sense of the objects which people have produced, in history, to represent or to form part of the world they experience. But the essence of culture is that it exists in the form of patterns of signification, and the reproduction, on film or elsewhere, of a cultural problematic such as seems to be Visconti's main present interest implies a concern with the problem of signification and discourse which is incompatible with any form of realist aesthetic. As I suggested above, when talking about *L'Etranger*, a film of the book cannot be a film of the things which the book appears to be about. It has to confront the book as an item of discourse, or, in simpler terms, as style. The same applies to Thomas Mann. To like Mann and to sympathise with what he stands for is one thing. To hope to reproduce this sympathy through a transposition into one's own work of Mannian values or of aspects of the Mannian thematic is another. The trick which makes this transposition appear feasible is a belief in realism and in Mann's status as a realist writer. Thus the representation in *The Damned* of the bourgeoisie and the bourgeois family as a cultural force draws heavily on a similar representation in Mann's *Buddenbrooks*. In terms of real history the claims made on behalf of an actually existing bourgeoisie are, doubtless, extremely mystifying, but aesthetically the transposition can be made (and, even better, can pass unadverted) because both *The Damned* and *Buddenbrooks* can claim, in their way, to be realist works. But any further dependence on Mann runs up against the fact that Mann stands for what he does by virtue of the kind of discourse he produces not only in the form of a cultural object (a book) but also as a discourse on culture itself. The kind of problems which Mann is dealing with clearly fascinate Visconti. Whether he is equipped, in view of his aesthetic inheritance, to restate these problems on film, is quite another question.

The argument so far is, to say the least, extremely prejudicial towards *Death in Venice*, the film in which Visconti reaches the culminating point of his identification with the Hegelian *Geist*. But *Death in Venice*, like all Visconti's films, is highly contradictory, and it is only fair to suspend judgment on the aspect of 'Kultur' and to start by examining other aspects of the film which co-exist uneasily with its cultural or culturalist pretensions. For there is a sense in which Luchino Visconti's *Morte a Venezia* can be read without reference to Thomas Mann's *Der Tod in Venedig* of which it is an adaptation and on which it provides a sort of commentary. It is such a reading which we will now attempt, if only to see how far it takes us.

It should be said at the outset that this is in no sense intended as a naïve reading of the film. It is not an attempted reading of the whole film such as might be made by someone who had never heard of Thomas Mann and did not know that the film was an adaptation of a pre-existing literary work. Such a reading could only be subjectivist and quite profoundly false, for reasons which should become clear.[7] What I have in mind is a partial reading, which deliberately abstracts as far as possible from the cultural overtones with which the film is beset and which concerns itself (again as far as possible) solely with the internal correlation of the immediate signifying attributes of the film as contained in the images, the dialogues and the sound track, without reference to external cultural determinants. For the purpose of this reading Venice is just a place, Gustav von Aschenbach is just a character, Mahler is just a composer, a look is just a look. Whatever further meanings these names or events may have had for Mann, or for Visconti, or for the spectator *moyen cultivé*, or for me for that matter, is a question to be integrated into the argument later. It is not a question of preferring a "cinematic" reading to a "literary" one, but a deliberate effort of abstraction in order to determine the precise place of cultural and quasi-literary discourse within the overall structure of the film.

The essential components of the film, on this reading, are a present time and a past time. In the present time there is seascape and townscape, a successful arrival and an abortive departure. There is a hotel with an international clientèle, at a short distance from the town. There are relationships between the guests, and there are words exchanged between the particular guest whose arrival we have watched and various people whose job it is to serve him. There is also an exchange of glances between this guest, a middle-aged man, and a fourteen-year-old boy who is also staying at the hotel. At the end of the film we see the middle-aged man die on the beach outside the hotel, facing out towards the sea across which he first arrived. In the past time, represented by a series of flashbacks, we see the same man, younger, in a variety of situations. We learn that he is a successful composer, that he has had a family life, that he has certain ideals both for his life and for his art. There is one seemingly casual link between the two time registers: the name of the prostitute whom he encounters in one of the flashbacks is Esmeralda, which is also the name of the boat on which he arrives in Venice in the main narrative.

It is clear that the scenes from past time are intended to illuminate and explain the significance of the events of the present. Certainly without the key that they provide the events in present time are singularly lacking in depth. But before using this key in order to open up the film and reveal whatever depth may lie behind the surface, it is worth analysing more closely the surface represented in the present-tense narrative.

In the course of the film the guest, Gustav von Aschenbach, is involved in a series of encounters. On the boat he is accosted by a strange drunken old man with a made-up face. Between the landing stage and the hotel he travels by gondola. The dialogue with the gondolier consists of an argument as to whether the gondolier should take him to the Lido or only to the steamboat landing. In the English-language version of the film this dialogue takes place in English. Meanwhile the gondolier is muttering to himself incomprehensibly in dialect. (One may take it that the English, and no doubt the German versions of the film are as authentic as the Italian, in which the same contrast exists, but is less marked.) On arrival at the hotel the guest is received with much bowing and scraping by the *maître d'hôtel*. He is treated as a rich and distinguished personage but does not seem to be much trusted or liked. Almost all the dialogues in which the guest is involved throughout the present-tense narrative of the film follow the pattern established in the opening scenes. He never speaks with his fellow guests, but only with people who are structurally in the position of servants or cast in a role of service and even servility. But the form of a master/slave relationship does not mean that the master controls the servants: on the contrary they control him. The gondolier takes him after all to the hotel, not just to the steamboat landing. The *maître d'hôtel* guides his movements and attempts to deceive him about the presence of plague in the city. An English clerk in Cook's tells him the truth, but in a way that seems more calculated to demonstrate the clerk's own erudition and the power of his fantasy than to impart useful advice. The barber who cuts Aschenbach's hair, shaves him, trims his moustache and finally dyes his hair and covers his face with a layer of make-up does so on the basis of no instructions from his client. The constant use of alien languages (at no time does Aschenbach exchange any words in German with fellow German speakers) and the alternation of servility and manipulation in which he is subjected establish a very sharp separation between Aschenbach and the world around him.

The separation between Aschenbach and his human and social context, it should be stressed, implies no metaphysics of alienation. It is specific to Aschenbach and has no echoes in the life around him which is crowded and gregarious. It also seems to characterise the present only, and not the past. Aschenbach comes to Venice alone and he dies there alone, but the sense of the event is given not by the emptiness but rather by the fullness of what surrounds him. The emptiness is between himself and the world, not in the world itself.

Besides separateness, or non-relatedness, another theme attached to the figure of Aschenbach is age, or rather the problem of ageing and agelessness. As well as the drunken old man who appears at the beginning there is another similar made-up figure in the film. This time it is (significantly) a musician, the leader of a band of strolling players who entertain the guests on the terrace outside the hotel. After he has finished playing and collected his money the musician retreats, facing the guests, singing a song whose vocal line consists entirely of raucous and mocking laughter. Later Aschenbach himself emerges from the barber's similarly made up and artificially rejuvenated. On his way home he collapses by a fountain and laughs gently to himself while the mask begins to peel and the make-up begins to run on his cheeks. Though the sense of this scene clearly has something to do with his feeling of failure as an artist, its main motif seems to be the incongruity of being both prematurely aged and disguised to look young, particularly in the light of his passion for Tadzio, the boy with whom, or with whose image, he has fallen in love.

Aschenbach's passion for the Polish boy Tadzio is the core of the film, and, in the way it is portrayed, is clearly inseparable from the representation of Aschenbach's separateness and from the theme of age and youth. Tadzio is on the verge of puberty: Aschenbach's condition can be not unfairly described as menopausal. The age gap which separates them is that of the entire time-span of adolescent and adult sexuality. But this difference in age is, if you like, merely a given fact. It establishes certain *a priori* limits to the kind of relationship possible between the characters, pedagogic or pederastic or whatever, according to taste. It is hardly an absolute barrier to the development of some sort of contact. What is not given *a priori* but emerges through the unfolding of the narrative is the perpetuation of Aschenbach's solitude. The same mechanisms which show Aschenbach's separateness from the ordinary world of the Venetians going about their business operate in intensified form in relationship to Tadzio. The boy is shown constantly surrounded by his family—mother, governess and sisters—or by friends of his own age. Aschenbach listens and observes. But his pleasure is constantly frustrated when, for example, from speaking French with the governess the family revert to incomprehensible Polish, or when from being the inviolate object of Aschenbach's contemplation Tadzio becomes a participant in a game from which the longing observer is excluded. When this happens Aschenbach can only avert his eyes.

The essence of Aschenbach's attitude to Tadzio is that it is voyeuristic. Whatever other frustrated desires may be present in the mind of the voyeur, the relationship he sets up with the object of his desire is in the first place one of seeing—of seeing and not being seen to see. Tadzio as the object of contemplation is also the object of a fantasy possession on the part of the older man. But the voyeur can possess his object only in fantasy and only as an object.

When Jasciu, Tadzio's slightly older companion, puts his arm round Tadzio's shoulder and Tadzio walks off with him, or when Tadzio returns Aschenbach's gaze with a look of equal intensity, the voyeur's spell is broken and he is brought face to face with the absurd logic of his own position. He wishes but he wishes he did not wish. However much he may make believe that his contemplation of Tadzio is that of the aesthete before a statue the fact is that he desires the statue to spring to life, that he desires this and yet cannot face the consequences of this happening. He cannot face the sight of Tadzio being the object of active affection for somebody else, nor the idea that Tadzio might return this affection. Nor can he bear any of the possible implications of Tadzio's smile directed towards himself. In short his desire is by definition impossible.

There remains however one possible way in which the conflict can be reconciled, and that is for Aschenbach to represent Tadzio to himself as a symbol. In this light Tadzio can represent for Aschenbach a child, and in particular the child he himself is shown in the flashback as having had but who died while still very young. Equally Tadzio can represent youth, basically Aschenbach's own lost youth, but also the state of transition from innocence to corruption. The presence of the plague, and of the *scirocco* blowing hot sultry air along the plague routes, contrasted with the implied Nordic purity of Tadzio (and of Aschenbach's past world), suggest a further, more objective symbolism. For Aschenbach Tadzio *is* the embodiment of certain ideas and possesses this symbolic value independently of his status as the object of voyeuristic fantasy.

But, but, but. In the film there is in fact a total disjunction between the possible levels of interpretation. If the present-tense narrative alone is taken into consideration, then there is only the voyeuristic relationship. Integration of the flashback suggests further possibilities of explanation for Aschenbach's obsession. Maybe he is not just a voyeur. Maybe there is some complicated process of sublimation at work. Maybe this tetchy old man has a mental and fantasy life richer and more intelligible than can be deduced from merely watching him lech after a pubescent boy in a provocative bathing costume. The problem is that the symbolic meanings which can be extracted from the interrelation of the two time levels do not succeed in making sense of the crypto-sexual relationship between old man and young boy, which remains, at best, merely pathetic. Nor, conversely, does the phenomenology of voyeurism as displayed in the present-tense narrative function as an illustration of any of the problems touched on in the flashback. The scenes from the past indicate various things about Aschenbach, for example that he is a puritan, that his artistic ideal is a music whose sources of inspiration are somehow spiritual and non-sensual and that the successful pursuit of this supposed ideal has left him dissatisfied. It is also suggested, fleetingly, that Tadzio, whom he appears to fantasise as an image of purity, also represents to him the dangers of sensuality, which, whether because of moral scruple or mere incapacity, he feels obliged to run away from. (This, at least, would appear to be the sense to be extracted from the cut from Tadzio picking out Beethoven's *Für Elise* on the piano to the same tune being played by the prostitute Esmeralda in the flashback.) Clearly there are connections of a kind between Tadzio, as symbol or as reality, and Aschenbach's past life, just as there is a connection of a kind between his crisis as a musician and the parody of himself that he encounters in the form of the strolling player. But there is no way of construing these connections except speculatively, for a very simple reason. None of the themes raised in the film receives any coherent treatment except by reference to the consciousness of Aschenbach, which is their only possible focus. But most of the time the themes are not focused. The style of representation is for the most part objective. The point of view is undiscriminating between the events and does not establish a privileged position for a narrator or even, except rarely, for the central character himself. The symbolic potential of the film is in consequence unrealised. The spectator is made aware that there could be meanings in the events and in the narration, but can never be quite clear what meanings or where to locate them. The film is obviously Art, and the central character is an Artist, so somewhere there must be Thought. But there isn't. There is, admittedly, pathos. But that is another matter entirely.

It says a lot for Mann's *novella* that the pathetic pastiche that Visconti has made of it is still capable of reproducing at least a few echoes of its original subtle discourse. For Visconti's *Morte a Venezia* is not merely an empty film but a pretentious film—pretentious and above all parasitic. The existence, alongside the film, of that minor miracle of discursive-narrative prose which is *Der Tod in Venedig*, seems to have dispensed Visconti from any attempt to produce a discourse of his own. In the event (frequent) of a void in the symbolic structure of the film, the spectator can mentally interpolate elements of the original *novella*. Failing knowledge of the *novella* there is at least the reassurance contained in the fact that it exists. The enormous 'art-déco' construction into which Visconti has inserted the washed-out figure of Gustav von Aschenbach, composer, evokes the world of a kind of decadentist literature which invests the whole enterprise with the Values of Culture. Little matter that these values are not really present.

Let us however turn to the *novella* and note some of its features. First Aschenbach is a writer, not a musician, and moreover a writer who has idealised and come to represent publicly certain models of culture and cultivated, restrained behaviour. Secondly the narrative structure allows for a constant interflow between Aschenbach's interior discourse, so obviously at odds with his infatuation with Tadzio, and the Mannian discourse which situates it and makes its significance explicit at a more general level. Thirdly Tadzio is very obviously the object of a projection on the part of Aschenbach. He represents almost before he exists. Aschenbach's story is, in the *novella*, the story of a cultural crisis, or, more accurately, of a crisis in ideology. The voyeuristic aspect of his attitude to Tadzio is an almost accidental by-product of the narrative technique, while the repressed pederastic element, so far from being the content of which voyeurism is the form, is merely the means through which Aschenbach becomes conscious of his own ideological limits and of the failure of his life-work. Right to the end of the story, however, Aschenbach remains a prisoner of Culture, of the same Culture of which he was a leading representative and which he himself had set up as a systematic defence against the real. Even the dream which reveals to him the erotic basis of his infatuation with the figure of Tadzio is cast in cultural terms, as a conflict between the Apollonian and the Dionysiac as modes of representation.

This imprisonment within a cultural, or culturalist, ideological problematic is typical of a number of Mann's characters, and can indeed be seen as characteristic of Mann himself. But the author is always that bit wiser than the characters he has created. It is not in the nature of his art to create characters which precisely express his own consciousness. Rather he poses problems (which are his own problems) through the creation of characters who express some or other aspect of the general problematic. These characters are constantly grappling with phantoms which are the consequence of their own ideological mode of representing reality to themselves. But they are not phantoms which can be easily exorcised, and Mann is no exorcist. His great strength as a writer lies in his awareness of the power of these phantoms, which collectively constitute the ideological universe of bourgeois society, and in his ability to manipulate them in a way which demonstrates both the coherence and the contradictions of the entity which we call culture. Basically Mann, unlike Musil,[9] is an idealist, who sees culture as an essence and who aspires to explain the world through its realisations in the realm of the Idea rather than to challenge the genesis of ideas in terms of their contradictions. At the same time, however, he does see that the contradictions exist. As an artist who writes about art he both criticises ideology and constantly reconstitutes it at a higher level. The Mannian character is unable to live his existence except soulfully and in the end is either paralysed or actually destroyed by the soul he has himself created for himself. The author presents this act of self-destruction sympathetically and yet ironically, proposing as a remedy to the mystified self-consciousness of the character only a higher degree of consciousness of his own limitations within the given cultural framework, not a dissolution of the mystified cultural consciousness itself.

Of all this, needless to say, barely a whiff in Visconti's rendering of the story. Culture is present, particularly in the flashback (which incidentally leans heavily on Mann's treatment of a musician hero in his *Dr Faustus*), but it is not seen problematically, only as a passively assimilated "value". By abolishing the structured discourse of the *novella*, with its twin foci in the mind of Aschenbach and in Mann's commentary on his cultural and sexual dilemma, Visconti has in a sense brought the story out of the clouds and down to earth and exposed the material, or rather the pseudo-ontological, content of Aschenbach's obsession. But this vulgar-materialist reduction of discourse to a level of landscape with figures does not demystify. It merely demonstrates incomprehension. To give but one example of the crassness of the adaptation, in the book the account of the spread of the plague is not given in direct speech but is part of the commentary. The clerk's words are rephrased, in a typical Mannian way, so as to express not only what has been said but also all the possible overtones of cultural significance which the particular listener, in this case the writer Aschenbach, or some other cultured person might attribute to them. They are also, very definitely, Mann's words. They represent an intervention of the author in his material, uniting what has been said and heard into the cultural discourse which the author wishes to share with his readers. In the film, pronounced by the clerk in the Cook's office, the words lack these resonances. They sound like a private culture-trip which frightens Aschenbach because of its strangeness and lack of relation to his own concerns. The words are there, but they might as well not be since destroying their original context has deprived them of their original meaning without creating an alternative, except at the most trivial level. Homage is paid to the literary genius of Thomas Mann, and, in its self-negating way, the scene is quite effective, but the reason why Mann's discourse as opposed to that of some other writer should be important and worth reproducing is totally and irrevocably lost. The film trades upon, and helps to perpetuate, respect for the values of Art while offering no reason why this Art should be taken even remotely seriously.

I am very conscious, as I write, that a few years ago I would not have expressed myself in this way about any Visconti film. If he had produced *Death in Venice* at the time when I was writing the first edition of this book I would undoubtedly have treated it more indulgently. I would probably have stressed Visconti's continuing technical mastery of the medium and the recurrence of *auteur* features familiar from the earlier films, the use of laughter, for example, or the assertion of the values of high culture against those of popular entertainment. But I no longer feel that technical and imaginative control (obtained, often enough, by the use of good actors and a good lighting-cameraman) or even authorship are values to be sought for in themselves. Recognised, yes: but not necessarily defended. Far more important, it seems to me, is the question of what meanings, and what order of meanings, can be conveyed in a work of art, and what basic choices an artist can make in relation to the linguistic material at his disposal. Questions of this order have been raised in the past five or six years with a frequency unprecedented in the history of the cinema. They have not been raised by Visconti. What Visconti has done has been to wander, blindfold, into areas being actively explored by other, maybe lesser, directors with their eyes open. Historically Visconti's place in the cinema pantheon seems to me secure, though I would not define it quite in the same way as I did five years ago. But his reputation, I suspect, will continue to depend on his first four films and hopefully also on the last film to be included in the first edition of this book, *Vaghe Stelle dell'Orsa*, which I am more and more convinced is his greatest single work. As for his latest work, it would be worse than unjust to regard it as the product of senile decline. Rather it represents an involution, brought about by an inability to resolve theoretical questions of what the film is supposed to do at a time when his imaginative ability to achieve certain practical effect is in no way impaired. *Death in Venice* is no product of babbling amateurism. It is, at times and in its own way, quite a brilliant movie. Unfortunately this brilliance is suspended on a void. Much of the abuse to which it is treated in the foregoing pages is due to the fact that it is brilliant and not to be lightly dismissed. If, instead, it has been heavily demolished, this is in part at least a sign of respect. The Fall of the Gods is not easily accomplished.

1. Not only is *Senso* by common consent regarded as one of Visconti's greatest films: it is also his most successful and creative adaptation. A sustained comparison between the film and Boito's *novella* is made in a research thesis by Ruth Kreitzman, *Rapporti tra film e narrativa nel cinema italiano*, Liverpool University 1972 (unpublished).

2. Written in 1953: p. 68 of Gonthier edition. Also, on p. 67: "Cette parole transparente, inaugurée par *L'Etranger* de Camus, accomplit un style de l'absence qui est presque une absence idéale du style; l'écriture se réduit alors à une sorte de mode négatif dans lequel les caractères sociaux ou mythiques d'un langage s'abolissent au profit d'un état de la forme."

3. Referred to by Lino Miccichè in his introduction to the script of *Death in Venice* (L. Visconti, *Morte a Venezia*, Cappelli 1971).

4. This may be the result of a cut in the English-language version.

5. See review of the film by Rosalind Delmar in *Monthly Film Bulletin*, May 1970.

6. For example when Herbert, the liberal (or "good") capitalist, acts as a mouthpiece for the view (shared by Visconti?) that the German bourgeoisie created Fascism as a kind of monster of Frankenstein in their efforts to avert the (lesser) danger of Social Democracy.

7. *Senso* might seem a partial refutation of this claim, as might one or two works of twentieth-century literature (Heinrich Mann, perhaps, if not Thomas). But in general I would argue (also for a hundred and one other reasons not gone into in this book) that the Marxist artist, to be consistent, has to remove himself at some distance from the sphere of realism, however "critical", in order to establish and to clarify his relationship with reality. Brecht is an obvious example, as is Mayakovsky.

8. The simplest way of summarising the case is to say that what matters first is what is in the film, not what A, B, or C gets out of it. We all bring our own cultural background to the interpretation of a film, and we all react differently. But what the film means is not the sum, or the mean, of all these subjective readings. This is not to deny people a right to their own opinion; just to assert that the critic's job is something other than acting as a mediator between the film and all the various opinions that may be formed of it. If the critic succeeds in showing that the film of *Death in Venice* is incomprehensible without reference to the book, this is, needless to say, a criticism of the film, not of the unprepared spectator.

9. The extraordinary thing about Robert Musil's *The Man without Qualities*, a book which can justifiably be compared with Mann's more

ponderous *œuvre*, is that it moves exclusively and one might almost say shamelessly within the realm of ideology, without the slightest pretence that this world of ideology is expressive of any historical essence. This lucid materialist position earns for it the spluttering ire of Lukács (*The Meaning of Contemporary Realism*, p. 31).

Filmography

Luchino Visconti

Born on 2 November 1906
He began his cinema career working for Jean Renoir on:
1936: LES BAS-FONDS
1937: UNE PARTIE DE CAMPAGNE
1940: LA TOSCA (begun by Renoir, finished by Koch)

Features
Ossessione (1942)

Production Company	ICI Rome
Producer	Libero Solaroli
Director	Luchino Visconti
Script	Mario Alicata, Antonio Pietrangeli, Gianni Puccini, Giuseppe de Santis, Luchino Visconti, from James Cain's novel *The Postman Always Rings Twice*
Directors of Photography	Aldo Tonti, Domenico Scala
Editor	Mario Serandrei
Art Director	Gino Rosati
Music	Giuseppe Rosati

Clara Calamai (*Giovanna*), Massimo Girotti (*Gino*), Juan de Landa (*The Husband*), Elia Marcuzzo (*Lo Spagnuolo*), Dhia Cristani (*Anita*), Vittorio Duse (*The Lorry Driver*), Michele Riccardini, Michele Sakara.

Locations: Ferrara and district, Ancona.
Running time: 135 mins. For details of its early censorship and production problems, see Gianni Puccini, "Il Venticinque Luglio del Cinema Italiano" in *Cinema Nuovo*, 1 December 1953.
Distributor: ICI (Italy).
Never shown commercially in Britain.

La Terra Trema (Episodio del Mare) (1947)

Production Company	Universalia
Producer	Salvo d'Angelo
Production Manager	Anna Davini
Director	Luchino Visconti
Assistant Directors	Francesco Rosi, Franco Zeffirelli
Script	Luchino Visconti
Director of Photography	G. R. Aldo
Camera Operator	Gianni di Venanzo
Editor	Mario Serandrei
Music	Willi Ferrero
Sound	Vittorio Trentino

Filmed on locations in Aci-Trezza, Sicily, with a cast of non-professionals.
Running time: 160 mins.
Distributor: Victor Film (Italy).
Never shown commercially in Britain.

Bellissima (1951)

Production Company	Bellissima Films
Producer	Salvo d'Angelo
Production Managers	Paolo Moffa, Vittorio Glori
Director	Luchino Visconti
Assistant Directors	Francesco Rosi, Franco Zeffirelli
Script	Suso Cecchi d'Amico, Francesco Rosi, Luchino Visconti, based on a story by Zavattini
Directors of Photography	Piero Portalupi, Paul Ronald
Camera Operators	Oberdan Troiani, Idelmo Simonelli
Editor	Mario Serandrei
Art Director	Gianno Polidori
Music	Franco Mannino
Costumes	Piero Tosi
Sound	Ovidio del Grande

Anna Magnani (*Maddalena Cecconi*), Walter Chiari (*Alberto Annovazzi*), Tina Apicella (*Maria Cecconi*), Gastone Renzelli (*Spartaco Cecconi*), Alessandro Blasetti (*himself*), Tecla Scarano (*Acting Teacher*), Lola Braccini (*Photographer's Wife*), Arturo Bragaglia (*Photographer*), Linda Sini (*Mimmetta*), Vittorio Glori, Iris, Geo Taparelli, Mario Chiari.

Running time: 113 mins.
Distributors: Cei Incom (Italy), Italian Films Export (U.S.A.), Regent (G.B.).
Shown in Britain in 1953, title BELLISSIMA.

Senso (1954)

Production Company	Lux Film
Producer	Domenico Forges Davanzati
Director	Luchino Visconti
Script	Luchino Visconti, Suso Cecchi d'Amico, assisted by G. Prosperi, C. Alianello, G. Bassani, from a *novella* by Camillo Boito
Directors of Photography	R. R. Aldo,★ Robert Krasker★
Camera Operators	Giuseppe Rotunno,★ Francesco Izzarelli
Colour Process	Technicolor
Art Directors	Ottavio Scotti, Gino Brosio
Music	Bruckner's seventh symphony. Verdi's *Il Trovatore*
Costumes	Marcel Escoffier, Piero Tosi
Sound	Vittorio Trentino

Alida Valli (*Countess Livia Serpieri*), Farley Granger (*Lieutenant Franz Mahler*), Massimo Girotti (*Marquis Roberto Ussoni*), Heinz Moog (*Count Serpieri*), Rina Morelli (*Laura*), Marcella Mariani (*The Prostitute*), Christian Marquand (*Bohemian Officer*), Tonio Selwart (*Colonel Kleist*), Cristoforo de Hartungen (*Commander at Venetian Square*), Tino Bianchi (*Meucci*), Sergio Fantoni (*Patriot*), Marianna Leibl (*Wife of Austrian General*), Ernst Nadherny, Goliarda Sapienza.

Location shots in Venice and the Villa di Valmarana.
Running time: 115 mins. Several scenes were cut at the early stages.
Text of one censored scene appears in *Image et Son*, April 1956.
Distributors: Lux (Italy), Archway (G.B.).
Appeared in Britain in 1957 in a dubbed version entitled THE WANTON COUNTESS with cuts amounting to a further 15 mins. English dialogue by Tennessee Williams and Paul Bowles.
★ Contributions of Directors of Photography were as follows:
Aldo: Internal and external shots of Villa di Valmarana (including granary sequence), the battle, the retreat.

Lo Straniero →

Krasker: Fenice Theatre, outdoor Venice scenes, indoor Venice scenes (Franz's various homes, the Serpieri house, General's quarters), denunciation scene, Livia in the carriage, Marquis Ussoni's home in Venice. Rotunno: Execution of Franz, Livia's journey by carriage (external shots), various external shots of Venice.

Le Notti Bianche (1957)

Production Companies	CIAS/Vides (Rome), Intermondia (Paris)
Producer	Franco Cristaldi
Production Manager	Pietro Notarianni
Director	Luchino Visconti
Script	Suso Cecchi d'Amico, Luchino Visconti, from a short story by Dostoievsky
Director of Photography	Giuseppe Rotunno
Camera Operator	Silvano Ippoliti
Editor	Mario Serandrei
Art Directors	Mario Chiari, assisted by Mario Garbuglia
Music	Nino Rota
Costumes	Piero Tosi
Choreography	Dick Sanders
Sound	Vittorio Trentino

Maria Schell (*Natalia*), Marcello Mastroianni (*Mario*), Jean Marais (*The Lodger*), Clara Calamai (*The Prostitute*), Giorgio Listuzzi, Marcella Rovena, Dick Sanders, Maria Zanolli.

Running time: 107 mins.
Distributors: Rank Film Distributors of Italy (Italy), Rank (G.B.).
Shown in Britain in 1958, entitled WHITE NIGHTS.

Rocco e i Suoi Fratelli (1960)

Production Company	Titanus/Films Marceau
Producer	Giuseppe Bordogni
Director	Luchino Visconti
Script	Luchino Visconti, Suso Cecchi d'Amico, Pasquale Festa Campanile, Massimo Franciosa, Enrico Medioli, based on the book by Giovanni Testori *Il Ponte della Ghisolfa*

Director of Photography	Giuseppe Rotunno
Camera Operators	Nino Cristiani, Silvano Ippoliti, Franco Delli Colli
Editor	Mario Serandrei
Art Director	Mario Garbuglia
Music	Nino Rota
Costumes	Piero Tosi
Sound	Giovanni Rossi

Alain Delon (*Rocco*), Renato Salvatori (*Simone*), Annie Girardot (*Nadia*), Katina Paxinou (*Rosaria*), Roger Hanin (*Morini*), Paolo Stoppa (*Boxing Impresario*), Suzy Delair (*Luisa*), Claudia Cardinale (*Ginetta*), Spiros Focas (*Vincenzo*), Rocco Vidolazzi (*Luca*), Corrado Pani (*Ivo*), Max Cartier (*Ciro*), Alessandra Panaro (*Ciro's Fiancée*), Claudia Mori, Adriana Asti (*Girls in the Dry-Cleaners*).

Shot on location in Milan and Rome.
Running time: 180 mins.
Distributors: Titanus (Italy), Regal International (G.B.).
Shown in Britain in 1961 as ROCCO AND HIS BROTHERS with 6 mins. cut.

Il Gattopardo (1963)

Production Companies	Titanus/SNPC/SGC
Producer	Goffredo Lombardo
Production Managers	Enzo Provenzale, Giorgio Adriani
Production Organiser	Pietro Notarianni
Director	Luchino Visconti
Script	Suso Cecchi d'Amico, Pasquale Festa Campanile, Enrico Medioli, Massimo Franciosa, Luchino Visconti, from the novel by Giuseppe Tomasi di Lampedusa
Director of Photography	Giuseppe Rotunno
Camera Operators	Nino Cristiani, Giuseppe Maccari, Enrico Cignitti
Colour Process	Technicolor
Editor	Mario Serandrei
Art Director	Mario Garbuglia
Music	Nino Rota and unpublished waltz by Verdi
Costumes	Piero Tosi
Sound	Mario Messina

213

Burt Lancaster (*Don Fabrizio, Prince of Salina*), Alain Delon (*Tancredi*), Claudia Cardinale (*Angelica Sedara*), Paolo Stoppa (*Don Calogero Sedara*), Rina Morelli (*Princess Maria Stella*), Serge Reggiani (*Don Ciccio Tumeo*), Romolo Valli (*Father Pirrone*), Leslie French (*Chevalley*), Ivo Garrani (*Colonel Pallavicino*), Mario Girotti (*Count Cavriaghi*), Pierre Clementi (*Francesco Paolo*), Lucilla Morlacchi (*Concetta*), Giuliano Gemma (*The Garibaldino General*), Ida Galli (*Carolina*), Ottavia Piccolo (*Caterina*), Carlo Valenzano (*Paolo*), Lola Braccini (*Donna Margherita*), Howard N. Rubien (*Don Diego*).

Locations: Sicily.
Running time: 205 mins.
Distributors: Titanus (Italy), Twentieth Century-Fox (U.S.A.), Twentieth Century-Fox (G.B.).
Shown in Britain in 1964, entitled THE LEOPARD, cut to 161 mins., in De Luxe colour and redubbed—for details, see article by Brenda Davies in *Sight and Sound* Spring 1964. And for Visconti's views on the alterations made see his letters to *The Times*, 17 December 1963, and *Sunday Times*, 27 October 1963.

Vaghe Stelle dell'Orsa (1965)

Production Company	Vides
Producer	Franco Cristaldi
General Production Organiser	Oscar Brazzi
Production Manager	Sergio Merolle
Director	Luchino Visconti
Script	Suso Cecchi d'Amico, Luchino Visconti, Enrico Medioli
Director of Photography	Armando Nannuzzi
Camera Operators	Nino Cristiani, Claudio Cirillo
Editor	Mario Serandrei
Art Director	Mario Garbuglia
Music	Prelude, Chorale and Fugue by César Franck
Costume	Bice Brichetto
Sound	Claudio Maielli

Claudia Cardinale (*Sandra*), Jean Sorel (*Gianni*), Michael Craig (*Andrew*), Marie Bell (*The Mother*), Renzo Ricci (*Gilardini*), Fred Williams (*Pietro Fornari*), Amalia Troiani (*Fosca*), Vittorio Manfrino, Renato Moretti, Giovanni Rovini, Paolo Pescini, Isacco Politi.

Locations: Volterra.
Running time: 100 mins.
Distributors: Columbia (Italy), Royal Film International (U.S.A.), Gala (G.B.).
Shown in Britain in 1965, entitled OF A THOUSAND DELIGHTS.
American title SANDRA.

Lo Straniero [English title: *The Stranger*] (1967)

Production Company	Dino De Laurentiis Cinematografica/Master Film (Rome)/Marianne Productions (Paris)/ Casbah Film (Algiers)
Producer	Dino De Laurentiis
Associate Producer	Pietro Notarianni
Production Manager	Mario Lupi
Director	Luchino Visconti
Assistant Directors	Rinaldo Ricci, Albino Cocchi
Script	Luchino Visconti, Suso Cecchi D'Amico, Georges Conchon. Based on the novel *L'Etranger* by Albert Camus
Co-adaptation	Emmanuel Robles
Director of Photography	Giuseppe Rotunno
Editor	Ruggero Mastroianni
Art Director	Mario Garbuglia
Music	Piero Piccioni
Musical Director	Bruno Nicolai
Sound	Vittorio Trentino

Marcello Mastroianni (*Meursault*), Anna Karina (*Marie Cardona*), Georges Wilson (*Examining Magistrate*), Bernard Blier (*Defence Counsel*), Jacques Herlin (*Director of Home*), Georges Géret (*Raymond Sintes*), Jean-Pierre Zola (*Employer*), Mimmo Palmara (*Masson*), Angela Luce (*Mme. Masson*), Bruno Cremer (*Priest*), Pierre Bertin (*Judge*), Marc Laurent (*Emmanuel*), Alfred Adam (*Prosecutor*), Vittorio Duse (*Lawyer*), Joseph Maréchal (*Salamano*), Saada Cheritel (*1st Arab*), Mohamed Ralem (*2nd Arab*), Brahim Hadjadj (*3rd Arab*).

La Caduta degli Dei [English title: *The Damned*] (1969)

Production Company	Pegaso Film (Rome)/Praesidens Film (Zurich)
Executive Producer	Pietro Notarianni
Producers	Alfredo Levy, Ever Haggiag
Production Manager	Giuseppe Bordogni

217

Director	Luchino Visconti
Assistant Directors	Albino Cocco, Ruggero Mastroianni
Script	Nicola Badalucco, Enrico Medioli, Luchino Visconti
Directors of Photography	Armando Nannuzzi, Pasquale De Santis
Editor	Ruggero Mastroianni
Art Directors	Pasquale Romano, Enzo Del Prato
Music/Musical Director	Maurice Jarre
Costumes	Piero Tosi
Sound	Vittorio Trentini

Dirk Bogarde (*Friedrich Bruckmann*), Ingrid Thulin (*Baroness Sophie*), Helmut Griem (*Aschenbach*), Helmut Berger (*Martin*), Renaud Verley (*Günther*), Umberto Orsini (*Herbert Thallman*), René Kolldehoff (*Baron Konstantin*), Albrecht Schonhals (*Baron Joachim von Essenbeck*), Nora Ricci (*Governess*), Irini Wanka (*Lisa Keller*), Valentina Ricci (*Thilda*), Karen Mittendorf (*Erika*), Florinda Bolkan (*Olga*), Charlotte Rampling (*Elisabeth Thallman*), Peter Dane, Claus Höhne.

Morte a Venezia [English title: *Death in Venice*] (1971)

Production Company	Alfa Cinematografica
Executive Producers	Mario Gallo, Robert Gordon Edwards
Producer	Luchino Visconti
Production Manager	Anna Davini
Director	Luchino Visconti
Assistant Director	Albino Cocco
Script	Luchino Visconti, Nicola Badalucco. Based on the novel by Thomas Mann
Director of Photography	Pasquale De Santis
Editor	Ruggero Mastroianni
Art Director	Ferdinanco Scarfiotti
Music	Gustav Mahler
Musical Director	Franco Mannino
Costumes	Piero Tosi
Sound	Vittorio Trentino

Dirk Bogarde (*Gustav von Aschenbach*), Björn Andresen (*Tadzio*), Silvana Mangano (*Tadzio's Mother*), Marisa Berenson (*Frau von Aschenbach*), Mark Burns (*Alfried*), Romolo Valli, Nora Ricci, Carole André, Leslie French, Franco Fabrizi, Antonio Appicella, Sergio Garfagnoli, Ciro Cristofoletti, Luigi Battaglia, Dominique Darel, Masha Predit.

Shorts
Giorni di Gloria (1945)

Production Company	Titanus
Director	Mario Serandrei, in collaboration with Luchino Visconti, Giuseppe de Santis, Marcello Pagliero
Camera Operators	Giovanni Pucci, Massimo Terzano and others
Commentary	Umberto Calosso

Distributor: Titanus (Italy).
Never shown commercially in Britain.

Appunti su un Fatto di Cronaca (1951)

Second number of a news film series directed and produced by Mario Ferreri and Riccardo Ghione

Director	Luchino Visconti
Commentary	Vasco Pratolini

Running time: 8 mins.

Siamo Donne (1953) Fifth Episode

Other episodes directed by Alfredo Guarini, Gianni Franciolini, Roberto Rossellini, Luigi Zampa

Production Company	Titanus Films Costellazione
Producer	Alfredo Guarini
Director	Luchino Visconti
Script	Cesare Zavattini, Suso Cecchi d'Amico
Director of Photography	Gabor Pogany
Editor	Mario Serandrei
Music	Alessandro Cicognini

Anna Magnani

Running time: 18 mins.
Distributors: Titanus (Italy), Gala/Cameo Poly.
Shown in Britain in 1954, entitled WE, THE WOMEN.

Boccaccio '70 (episode *Il Lavoro*) (1962)

Other episodes directed by De Sica and Fellini

Production Companies	Concordia Compagnia Cinematografica/ Cineriz (Rome) and Francinex/Gray Films (Paris)
Producers	Carlo Ponti, Antonio Cervi
Director	Luchino Visconti
Script	Suso Cecchi d'Amico, Luchino Visconti, from an idea by Cesare Zavattini based on Maupassant's short story *Au Bord du Lit*
Director of Photography	Giuseppe Rotunno
Colour Process	Eastmancolour
Editor	Mario Serandrei
Art Director	Mario Garbuglia
Music	Nino Rota

Romy Schneider (*Pupe*), Tomas Milian (*The Count*), Romolo Valli (*The Lawyer*), Paolo Stoppa, Amedeo Girard.

Running time: 46 mins.

Distributors: Cineriz (Italy), Embassy Pictures (U.S.A.), Twentieth Century-Fox (G.B.).

Shown in Britain in 1963, film entitled BOCCACCIO'70, Visconti episode entitled THE JOB.

Le Streghe (episode *Le Strega Bruciata Viva*) (1966)

Other episodes by Mauro Bolognini, Pier Paolo Pasolini, Franco Rossi, Vittorio de Sica

Production Company	Dino de Laurentiis Cinematografica
Director	Luchino Visconti
Script	Giuseppe Patroni Griffi, with Cesare Zavattini
Director of Photography	Giuseppe Rotunno
Colour Process	Technicolor
Editor	Mario Serandrei
Music	Piero Piccioni

Silvana Mangano (*Gloria*), Annie Girardot (*Valeria*), Francisco Rabal (*Valeria's Husband*), Massimo Girotti (*Sporting Gentleman*).

Not yet shown commercially.

Acknowledgements

I should like to thank all those who have assisted me in the preparation of this book: the staff of the B.F.I. and N.F.T. for their help
in providing information and in enabling me to see copies of all
Visconti's films available in this country; Avv. Livio Bozzini and
Franca Alberici of Unitalia-film, Fausto Montesanti and the staff
of the Centro Sperimentale in Rome for help and information
when I was in Italy; Luchino Visconti for taking time off from
Lo Straniero to talk to me about his work; and Rosalind Delmar
for moral and material support and constructive criticism at all
times.

As far as books and articles are concerned my main debt is to the
printed scripts of Visconti's later films published by Cappelli, and
to the issue of *Premier Plan* (no. 17) devoted to Visconti's work up
to *Rocco and his Brothers*.

Stills are reproduced by courtesy of Paramount, Dino de
Laurentiis, Gala and Twentieth Century-Fox.

G.N.-S.